Citizen Participation in America

To Joan

Contents

Preface

In the past decade, there has been a rapidly growing interest in the phenomenon of citizen participation among government officials, citizen leaders, and scholars. During this period a great deal of literature has been produced from many quarters. This literature has been disparate and multidisciplinary. For the most part, it has fallen into the four general areas of democratic theory, studies of political behavior, community development and citizen action, and government-initiated citizen involvement. Each of these areas possesses distinctive traditions, interests, and approaches to the subject of citizen participation. Despite these different orientations, common themes and interrelated issues concerning citizen participation are found in these different approaches. This book is unique in that it approaches the subject of citizen participation from an integrative perspective that seeks to consider and draw upon these different approaches while identifying common and interrelated issues.

This book is intended for a general audience of citizen leaders, government officials, and scholars. A direct purpose, also, was to provide background materials for the National Conference on Citizen Participation in Washington, D.C., in September 1978, sponsored by the Lincoln Filene Center for Citizenship and Public Affairs, Tufts University, and cosponsored by Common Cause, the Interagency Council on Citizen Participation, the League of Women Voters Education Fund, the National Association of Neighborhoods, the National League of Cities, the National Municipal League, the National Urban League, and the United Way of America. It is intended that the book will provide a common frame of reference in addressing critical issues of theory and practice concerning citizen participation.

Preparation of this book required stringent deadlines and dedicated cooperation from the publisher, authors, and support staff at the Lincoln Filene Center. The commitment and discipline of all the authors has been extraordinary. Since these are all original essays, the authors were faced with an enormous creative challenge under severe time constraints. Not only did they meet this challenge, but they did so with grace and style. So, to Barry, John, Nelson, David, Janice, Tony, Jerry, and Judy, I want to express my deep gratitude and respect. One could not hope for a finer group of colleagues.

The production of a final manuscript is an arduous task. It requires countless hours of typing, editing, rewriting, and retyping. When time is at a premium, these are not always the most pleasant of tasks. However, when the right people are involved, what could be a carnival of conflict and disorder can be an experience of satisfying collaboration. Thanks to my colleagues at the Lincoln Filene Center, the latter has been the case in completing this book. I am most appreciative of the commitment, competence, and good nature of Mary Keating, Sandra Lee Ross, Virginia O'Neil, and Nancy Sartanowicz in preparing the manuscript. I am also very thankful to Miss Miriam C. Berry for her outstanding editorial assistance. The interest and commitment to this project of my close colleague, Francis H. Duehay, Executive Director of the Lincoln Filene Center, has meant a great deal, and I am grateful to him and to the officers of the Civic Education Foundation, which governs the Lincoln Filene Center, for their support.

Finally, I am most grateful to my wife, Joan, and our children, Todd, Heather, and Dean, for their sacrifices and patience while this book was being completed.

Stuart Langton
Lincoln Filene Center for
   Citizenship and Public Affairs
Tufts University
Medford, Massachusetts

Citizen Participation in America

1

Citizen Participation in America: Current Reflections on the State of the Art

Stuart Langton

The 1970s have been marked by a paradox in civic attitudes and behavior in America. We have witnessed growing reflections of citizen alienation, distrust, and withdrawal; however, we have seen also an explosion in citizen organizations and public interest groups and a multitude of efforts to make government more accessible, accountable, and responsive to citizens. While voter turnout, political-party affiliation, and public confidence continue to decline, special-interest politics accelerates, and a surprising percentage of people reflect the attitude that they would be willing to be involved in some form of political action in their communities.[1] As evidence of citizen apathy mounts, so does evidence indicating a democratic resurgence. While the literature of a new narcissism flourishes among the public, so does literature about public affairs. Although some commentators proclaim that a new cynicism abounds, others herald the arrival of a new populism. So it seems that America is both "turned off" and "turned on" to democratic governance at the same time.

Surface reflection may suggest that these are contradictory and unrelated forces, but it is more likely that they are two sides of the same coin. What this paradox does indicate are two different responses to political alienation in America. As confidence in and respect for government have declined, a "passivity-participation syndrome" has emerged. Quite simply, withdrawal and participation have become two predominant ways of acting upon dissatisfaction with government and society.

The Rise of Dual Citizen-Participation Movements

What is distinctive about the participatory response to government in America is its dual impulse: the demands for more citizen participation in government have come from government officials as well as from citizens. While many citizens have organized to influence and improve government, many officials have attempted to make government more accessible and responsive to citizens. Consequently, two citizen-participation movements have grown simultaneously in the last decade. The citizen-initiated movement has stressed the importance of citizen action to influence and monitor government. This citizen-action movement has included grassroots

1

organizations, public-interest groups, consumer groups, voluntary service organizations, and the like. The government-initiated movement has stressed the importance of involving citizens in improving and gaining support for administrative decisions and government programs. This citizen-involvement movement has given rise to the widespread practice of legislative mandating of citizen participation. As a result, countless rules and regulations for citizen participation now exist at all levels of government, and a growing cadre of specialists has been created to implement them.

The growth of these two citizen-participation movements confirms, in the American context at least, what Almond and Verba noted 15 years ago: "If there is a political revolution going on throughout the world, it is what might be called the participation explosion."[2] Since this observation was made, there has been *additional* quantum growth in participation in American government; and today, citizen participation represents an extremely dynamic, diverse, and pervasive force in our society.

The Citizen-Action Movement

While it is not possible to estimate accurately the number of citizen-action organizations that have arisen in the past several decades, there are a few estimates that indicate the scope of this movement. For example, Janice Perlman notes, in chapter 6, that the National Commission on Neighborhoods has identified more than 8,000 grassroot neighborhood organizations in the United States, and that in New York alone there are more than 10,000 block associations. In his 1972-1973 study, Jeffrey Berry noted that he had identified more than 100 national public-interest groups with offices in Washington, D.C.[3] The Office of Consumer Affairs of the U.S. Department of Health, Education and Welfare has estimated that there are more than 450 consumer groups in the nation.[4] The National Alliance for Volunteerism has established a consortium of 19 voluntary organizations for advocacy purposes.[5] The United Way of America has initiated a similar consortium, with 48 member organizations.[6] It has been estimated that there are approximately 350 environmental-action organizations[7] and 650 cases of citizen-initiated environmental litigation.[8] The Office of Neighborhoods, Voluntary Associations, and Consumer Affairs of the U.S. Department of Housing and Urban Development has identified nearly 15,000 consumer and citizen groups.[9] There are nearly 500 senior-citizen centers and clubs in the United States, many of which are engaged in advocacy efforts.[10] And there are more than 850 mental-health associations, most of which seek to influence government policy and programs.[11]

The number of initiatives undertaken by citizen-action groups in the past decade has been enormous and would require volumes to describe. Nonetheless, the impact of this movement is evident in the variety of substantial reforms that have taken place in government in recent years as a result of strong citizen action. Sunshine laws, financial disclosure laws, freedom of information legislation, consumer-rights legislation, and lobbyist registration requirements are but a few results of sustained citizen action at the federal and state levels. In addition, one could catalog countless instances in which citizen action has led to neighborhood revitalization, suspension of utility-rate increases, abandonment of highway construction projects, improvement in health facilities, cessation of nuclear power-plant construction, product-safety improvements, and discontinuance of discriminatory practices.

Whether general or specific, any tabulation of the recent efforts of the citizen-action movement demonstrates its extraordinary significance as a social force in our time. Further, even a cursory examination of this movement should dispel the myth that citizen action is essentially negative and obstructionist in nature. In truth, the citizen-action movement is a very broad spectrum of citizen response to many different political and social problems. While citizen action has often blocked government action, it has to an equal extent led to positive improvements and the establishment of long-needed government reform.

The Citizen-Involvement Movement

As dramatic as the growth of the citizen-action movement has been, the growth of the citizen-involvement movement has been equally significant. For example, it was only 30 years ago that the first federal administrative requirements for citizen involvement were established in the Administrative Procedures Act. Today, there are hundreds of requirements and regulations for citizen participation, many of which have been recently identified in a study by the Community Services Administration.[12]

Almost all new, major federal legislative programs contain citizen-participation requirements (for example, Airport and Airways Development Act, Federal Water Pollution Control Act, Coastal Zone Management Act, Energy Reorganization Act, and Housing and Community Development Act); and many programs, such as revenue sharing (State and Local Assistance Act of 1972), have been amended to include provisions for citizen participation.[13]

In the past several years, a number of programs have been undertaken that illustrate the extent and vitality of the federal commitment to citizen involvement. In 1976, for example, the largest agency of the federal government, the Department of Health, Education, and Welfare, initiated a program to strengthen citizen involvement within the agency. In 1978, the newest federal agency, the Department of Energy (DOE), has been developing plans for a citizen-participation program and has engaged two citizen-action groups, the Energy Policy Task Force and the Consumer Federation of America, to help design a system for funding public participation in DOE proceedings. In an attempt to encourage citizen involvement, several federal agencies (such as the Federal Trade Commission, the Consumer Product Safety Commission, the Food and Drug Administration, the Environmental Protection Agency, the Civil Aeronautics Board, and the National Highway Safety Administration) have developed experimental programs to reimburse citizen groups for participation in agency proceedings. Recently, the National Oceanic and Atmospheric Administration published rules and regulations to establish such a reimbursement program.[14] Meanwhile, Senators Edward M. Kennedy and Charles McC. Mathias have introduced a Bill, S.270, The Public Participation in Federal Agency Proceedings Act, which would "provide financial assistance to facilitate participation by citizens who can make important contributions to agency proceedings. . . . the bill permits Federal Courts to reimburse persons who bring successful lawsuits to challenge agency decisions . . . where a Court concludes that the action vindicates important public interests."[15] If this bill passes, its potential impact on citizen-action groups and all government agencies could be deeply significant.

Within the federal government, there are innumerable practical attempts to increase citizen involvement. To cite but a few examples: At the congressional level, Congressman Wyche Fowler of Georgia has developed a program in which people in his district (Atlanta) meet to identify goals and priorities; Congressman Charlie Rose of North Carolina has established a survey program in which his constituents identify quality-of-life preferences and federal spending priorities; scores of senators and House members are holding "town meetings" to inform and receive feedback from constituents; and the Senate of late has broken a long tradition by broadcasting its proceedings in the debate over the Panama Canal treaties. At the agency level, the Army Corps of Engineers has experimented with innovative public meeting programs and has undertaken an extensive public-involvement training program for agency personnel; the National Science Foundation has developed a Science for Citizens Program to improve citizen capacity in dealing with scientific and technological issues; the Environmental Protection Agency employs specialists to establish citizen-participation programs through its regional offices; the National Park Service has developed an "Inform and Involve" Program to increase citizen involvement in agency proceedings; and more than 200 professionals from various federal agencies have formed the Interagency Council on Citizen Participation.

At the executive level, the Carter administration has reflected a growing concern about citizen participation. For example, on March 23, 1978, the president issued an executive order entitled "Improving Government Relations" in which "opportunities for public participation" were ordered.[16] At the same time, citizen participation was being studied as a part of the president's reorganization program, and shortly thereafter the president's Office of Public Liaison began a study of citizen participation in agency decision making. On March 27, 1978, the president announced his urban policy and placed considerable emphasis on the importance of involving citizens at the neighborhood and community levels as a part of that policy.[17] On April 27, a memorandum was issued by the president announcing his "firm commitment to consumer involvement in government" and directing Esther Peterson, his special assistant for consumer affairs, to further assure consumer involvement in agency decision making."[18]

The growth of the citizen-involvement movement has not been confined to the federal level, as commitment at the state and local levels has been widespread. As an example, a 1975 study of one state, the Commonwealth of Pennsylvania, indicated more than 165 statutes requiring advisory committeees and public hearings. In surveying only nine agencies of government, the study found: "There may be as many as 700 different brochures published among the nine agencies, 30 regularly published newsletters with a total distribution of more than two million, over 500 special reports available upon request, and a combined total of approximately 3,500 news releases. There may be as many as 800 conferences, workshops, and courses provided to the general public among the nine agencies, and it is estimated that as many as 600 hearings and public meetings are held each year among the agencies."[19] Based on estimates of agency budgets committed to carrying out citizen-participation activities, the study suggested that as much as $50 million to $100 million might be spent in one year to carry out citizen-participation activities among Pennsylvania state agencies.

More than half of the states have some mechanism or special office, usually within the executive branch, to coordinate citizen involvement at the state level of government.[20] Some examples of this are the Governor's Action Center in Pennsylvania, the Governor's Office of Citizen Affairs in North Carolina, and the Department of Public Advocate in New Jersey. In addition to regular citizen involvement in agency proceedings, a number of states, such as Washington, Oregon, Georgia, Minnesota, Hawaii, and Massachusetts, have established special "goals" programs in which citizens are involved in identifying future priorities for the state.

The goals-program approach has also been implemented successfully at the local level in a number of cities, such as Dallas, Fort Worth, and Atlanta. In addition, hundreds of cities have established citizen advisory groups and neighborhood councils. In more than forty cities, neighborhood associations have been given discretionary power by the city to plan, implement, and/or evaluate programs for the neighborhood.[21] And several hundred communities utilize different kinds of ombudsmen programs to assist and involve citizens.[22]

Citizen Participation as a Response to Historic Needs

What has caused this quantum growth in citizen participation? Among the many causes that could be cited, three of historical significance illustrate the multiple functions that citizen participation performs in American government today.

The Decline of Mediating Institutions

The alienating conditions of modern bureaucracy and the alienating consequences of mass-industrialized society have been clear since the analyses of Max Weber, Emile Durkheim, and Ferdinand Tönnies. Although these forces have been present in America, mediating institutions, such as the church, political parties, and fraternal organizations, have helped to reconcile individuals to them. In this capacity, these institutions have helped to sustain pluralism, develop consensus, and provide social mobility.

In the past several decades, the influence of these mediating institutions has declined significantly, and this has led to an erosion in the traditional source of consensus making. As a result, it is now difficult to build political consensus during a period in which a multitude of critical choices must be made. In response, citizen participation is often viewed as an alternative means to build consensus. Whether or not citizen participation really facilitates consensus and, if so, under what conditions, are unresolved questions. Nonetheless, citizen participation today serves as an experimental alternative to compensate for the decline in traditional consensus making.

The Rise of the Bureaucratic Estate

Population growth, technology, and affluence have created a complex set of problems that places immense regulatory and service demands upon all levels of government. In meeting these demands, an enormous growth of government bureaucracy has taken place, and today government agencies are required to make a vast array of administrative decisions. This has led to the assumption of tremendous discretionary power in decision making among these agencies, and as a result, the civil service has practically become a fourth estate of government.

This historical development has created two important needs. First, there is an ever-present danger that administrative agencies may exceed or abuse their discretionary power. In this sense, the regulators need regulating. Although legislatures have responsibility for doing this, they can't do it as a practical matter. They have too much legislative work and the administrative bureaucracy has grown too large for them to monitor. Therefore, citizen participation has developed as an alternative means of monitoring government agencies.

Second, government agencies are not entirely comfortable with their discretionary power. Bureaucrats know that they are paid by taxpayers and are overseen by elected officials. Therefore, they are reluctant to make unpopular and controversial decisions. Unfortunately, this is not always possible, and as a result, justification and support for difficult decisions becomes a matter of critical importance to them. So, to reduce the potential of unpopular or questionable decisions, agencies frequently use citizen participation as a means of improving, justifying, and developing support for their decisions.

These two points illustrate a significant polarity in the meaning of citizen participation in the life of a government agency. On the one hand, citizen participation is a control mechanism when citizens perform a monitoring or "watchdog" function. On the other hand, citizen participation provides an assistance function regarding agency decisions. Ironically, citizen participation may represent either a threat or a way of reducing threats to an agency. It is not surprising to find, therefore, that many government officials are exceedingly ambivalent about it.

The Impact of Mass Media

A third significant historical factor that has stimulated the growth of citizen participation is the rise in influence of the mass media. Because of the communication revolution that has taken place throughout the world, today more information is available to more people in more ways and at more times than ever before. A consequence of this is that abuse of power, error, or poor performance by government agencies or officials is rapidly communicated to the public in many forms. Therefore, to many officials it seems that we live in an era of government by fishbowl.

The communication revolution has stimulated a heightened degree of citizen participation by making more people aware of more problems associated with government. This has resulted in a greater degree of citizen action at all levels of government and a broadening of the franchises for government reform to an ever-expanding group of citizens. In this sense, the use of mass media has sponsored another function of citizen participation—to serve as a means of government reform. Whether or not there are excesses and unanticipated consequences of this movement will remain to be seen. Whatever the case, given the dominance of media in our society and the ever-growing number of problems that government must address, it is doubtful that the impulse for government reform among citizens will abate.

These historical vignettes suggest two important things about citizen participation. One is that citizen participation is a multifaceted phenomenon that performs many functions. It is used as a means to build consensus, to monitor administrative agencies, to assist administrative agencies, and to initiate government reform. Further, all of these functions have grown in response to historical needs that have become more intense in recent years. Therefore, it is most likely that citizen participation will continue to grow in importance as a means of preserving and improving democratic practice in America.

Dominant Questions about Citizen Participation

The rapid growth of citizen participation has generated a formidable array of unanswered questions. While considerable information and insight abound, citizen participation is a subject that is marked by critical questions rather than decisive answers. At best, understanding and knowledge about citizen participation is uneven and incomplete, and an overload of challenging questions prevails.

Despite the multitude of specific questions about citizen participation, two dominant general questions recur and need to be addressed continuously. One is concerned with quantity, or the appropriate extent or limit of citizen participation; and the other is concerned with quality.

The Limits of Citizen Participation

The question of appropriate limits of citizen participation in government has long been a critical issue in democratic theory. Whether or not extensive participation leads to democratic distemper or vitality continues as a fundamental issue today. While this issue will undoubtedly continue to attract theoretical speculation, it is more likely and more important that it be addressed as an empirical question. In particular, it will be necessary to determine what the results of citizen participation are on the attitudes and behavior of citizens as well as on the functioning of government agencies. Such inquiry must include consideration of how participation influences citizens' sense of self-worth and efficacy as well as their sense of confidence, satisfaction, and commitment to the state. In addition, it should be determined what impact citizen participation has on the morale and performance of government officials as well as on the practices of the agencies.

Because of the multiple functions that citizen participation performs in contemporary democratic practice, the question of the appropriate limits of citizen participation cannot be adequately addressed without considering related questions about democratic functioning. For example, if citizen involvement is used as a means to generate consensus, it will only be possible to judge how extensively it should be used for this purpose by comparing it with other ways of building consensus. The same can be said in regard to the functions of improving administrative decision making or monitoring government agencies. Quite simply, if better means can be found, then the use of citizen involvement should be limited. If better means cannot be found or improved, then citizen involvement should be employed more extensively. In this regard, consideration of the extent of citizen participation must take place in the context of a more general evaluation of the health and efficacy of democratic institutions and practices in specific situations. Therefore, citizen participation should be viewed as either an alternative or a complementary means of improving democratic governance.

The Quality of Citizen Participation

An elected official once remarked to me, "There is good citizen participation and there is bad citizen participation, and until I see more of the former I will think of it in terms of the latter." It may well be that unsuccessful examples of citizen participation far outnumber successful ones, or it may be that criteria for determining success have been inadequate and misleading. Whatever the case, the question of the qualitative assessment and understanding of citizen participation needs to be given serious consideration. To address this question, attention must be given to two tasks that have seldom been undertaken.

The first task is to develop criteria for evaluating citizen participation according to the various functions it serves. In this respect, it will be necessary to identify different levels of success and to think in terms of differential outcomes.

The second task is to increase understanding of the conditions that encourage or inhibit the achievement of successful citizen participation. Among the many issues that need to be considered in this regard are the following:

1. *Citizenship education:* What capacities do citizens need in order to participate effectively? What knowledge, attitudes, and skills are required? In what ways can these capacities be best developed among youth and adults?

2. *Elitism:* Are elites inevitable in citizen-participation activities? In what ways are elites functional and dysfunctional? Are there different types of elites? Are there distinct attitudes and behaviors among elite groups that facilitate or undermine participation of larger numbers of citizens?

3. *Technological complexity:* To what extent and under what conditions should citizens be expected to deal with complex and technical decisions? What methods increase citizen understanding of such issues?

4. *Financing:* To what extent and in what ways is financing an important factor in citizen participation? Are there any workable formulas concerning the necessary costs for successful citizen-participation activities? What principles and procedures are necessary to guide effectively the financing of citizen-participation efforts?

5. *Government agency behavior:* What practices and procedures on the part of government agencies encourage and discourage successful participation? What organizational innovations are particularly helpful? What knowledge, skills, and attitudes are needed by agency personnel to encourage successful citizen participation? How can these capacities be developed?

6. *Representativeness:* In what instances is it necessary to seek broad-based representation in citizen participation? What methods encourage representative participation? What procedures encourage the participation of groups that are often unrepresented?

While many other important questions about citizen participation could be identified, these constitute some of the critical ones that should be part of any agenda for inquiry. In the following pages, many of these questions will be considered. Realistically, a short book of essays cannot do justice to the many critical questions about citizen participation that deserve thoughtful analysis at this time. Therefore, these essays seek to provide a framework for better understanding of many of these questions. In this sense the book is offered as an invitation to further inquiry to those who share a concern about the meaning of citizen participation in the late twentieth century.

Notes

1. George Gallup, "Strong Neighborhoods Offer Hope for the Nation's Citizen," *The Gallup Poll* (Sunday, March 5, 1978). In this poll 89% of the urban residents polled indicated willingness to engage in some form of political action in their community.

2. Gabriel A. Almond and Sidney Verba, *The Civic Culture: Political Attitudes and Democracy in Five Nations* (Princeton: Princeton University Press, 1963), p. 4.

3. Jeffrey M. Berry, *Lobbying for the People: The Political Behavior of Public Interest Groups* (Princeton: Princeton University Press, 1977).

4. *Directory of Consumer Organizations* (Washington: Office of Consumer Affairs, U.S. Department of Health, Education, and Welfare, October 1976).

5. Information provided by the National Association for Voluntarism.

6. Coalition of National Voluntary Organizations, 1214 16th Street, Washington, D.C. 20036.

7. *Conservation Directory* (Washington: The National Wildlife Federation).

8. Information provided by the Environmental Law Institute, Washington, D.C.

9. Information provided by the Office of Neighborhoods, Voluntary Associations, and Consumer Affairs, U.S. Department of Housing and Urban Development.

10. *Senior Citizen Centers: A Report of Senior Group Programs in America* (Washington: National Council on Aging, 1975).

11. Information provided by the National Association of Mental Health.

12. *Citizen Participation* (Washington: Community Services Administration, January 1978).

13. For general discussion of this issue see Steven D. Rudman and Duane J. Ruffner, *Citizen Participation, General Revenue Sharing, and the Municipal Budget Process* (Claremont, Calif.: Claremont Graduate School Public Policy Studies, 1977).

14. *Federal Register,* Vol. 43, No. 81 (Wednesday, April 26, 1978); Chapter IX, National Oceanic and Atmospheric Administration, Department of Commerce; Part 904, Financial Compensation of Participation in Administrative Proceedings, p. 17806 ff.

15. Hearings Before the Subcommittee on Administrative Practice and Procedure of the Committee on the Judiciary of the United States Senate, on a Bill, S.270, The Public Participation in Federal Agency Proceedings Act of 1977 (Washington: U.S. Government Printing Office, 1977), Part 1, p. 1.

16. Jimmy Carter, *The White House* (Executive Order, Improving Government Regulations, Section 2, Opportunity for Public Participation, March 23, 1978).

17. Jimmy Carter, "New Partnership to Preserve American Communities," The White House (Washington: March 27, 1978).

18. Jimmy Carter, Memorandum for the Heads of Departments and Agencies, The White House (Washington: April 27, 1978).

19. Stuart Langton & Associates, *A Survey of Citizen Participation Re-*

quirements and Activities among Major State Agencies of the Commonwealth of Pennsylvania (Fremont, N.H.: 1976).

20. Ibid.

21. Information provided by the National Association of Neighborhoods, Washington, D.C.

22. Information provided by Bernard Frank, Chairman, Ombudsman Committee, International Bar Association, Allentown, Pa.

2

What is Citizen Participation?

Stuart Langton

The definition and analysis of citizen participation is a formidable task. As a community organizer recently said to me, it is like "grabbing hold of a marshmallow; it is more rhetoric than reality." Yet whatever problems there may be with the reality of citizen participation, there are equal problems with the rhetoric. Like a marshmallow, definitions and analyses of citizen participation have been all too soft, pliable, and susceptible to dissolution under the heat of careful scrutiny. As Spiegel and Mittenthal acknowledged a decade ago: "Truly the more one explores the endless ramifications of citizen participation, the more one appreciates the old adage of 'having a tiger by the tail.' Every effort to reduce its protean-like substance to a definable, systematic and comprehensible body of thought is resisted by inherent dilemmas—contradictions between myth and reality and even different sets of observable social phenomenon. Citizen participation virtually defies generalizations and delights in reducing abstractions to dust."[1]

Given this inescapable difficulty, it is not surprising that citizen participation means different things to people and that confusion and ambiguity are common in discussions about it. Despite this, the term *citizen participation* and the concept retain a remarkable attraction for a number of people. The idea seems to mean something important to them. In this sense, citizen participation seems to be what C.L. Stevenson has referred to as an "emotive term"[2] that possesses the power of what Ernst Cassirer has ascribed to a metaphor.[3]

Undoubtedly, it is the diverse, emotive, and metaphorical quality of citizen participation that has made many government officials, citizen leaders, and scholars uneasy about it. To some it is too wedded to the political activism of the 1960s and the growing demand for more power among the poor and minorities. To others, it is too general and vague. And to still others, it does not reflect adequately the limited and controlled degree of involvement that is desired in administrative decision making with government agencies. Accordingly, corollary terms, such as citizen involvement, public participation, public involvement, citizen action, and political participation, have grown in popularity in the past decade.

In the light of this trend, one wonders whether the term *citizen participation* has any meaningful use at all, and, if so, what the relation of these corollary terms is to it. I should like to argue that the term *citizen par-*

13

ticipation, and the concept it represents, does have a distinct and important meaning and that several of the other terms in current use, such as citizen action and citizen involvement, represent important types of citizen participation.

From Symbol to Function: The Metamorphosis of the Concept of Citizen Participation

It is only during the past several decades that the term citizen participation has been coined into popular use. During this relatively brief history, the concept of citizen participation has been associated with three developments that have had a profound impact on democratic theory and practice in the United States. The first of these was the civil rights movement, which heightened the aspiration of minority and poor persons and gave rise to the war on poverty, with its emphasis on "maximum feasible participation." The second development is the rapid and substantial growth of the public-interest movement, with its emphasis on openness, access, and accountability in government. The third is the much less heralded, but highly pervasive, movement among government agencies to inform citizens better and involve them more in planning and decision making.

The causes and implications of the powerful democratic resurgence in America represented by these three movements are still not fully clear. Undoubtedly, questions about this will dominate political theory, research, and practice for years to come. Meanwhile, the term *citizen participation* remains associated with these developments and recurs constantly in policy and programmatic responses to them.

Because of these developments, the concept of citizen participation is undergoing a significant metamorphosis as interest grows in functional analysis and application. This is evident, for example, as government agencies establish citizen-participation policies, regulations, and procedures, and as a growing number of scholars study the concept. Consequently, citizen participation is changing from a symbolic to a functional concept, and so we are witnessing a heightened need for clearer analysis of it.

While some may fear that analysis may rob the concept of citizen participation of some of its vitality and influence, there are others who feel that the lack of analysis will weaken efforts to implement it. Both concerns are legitimate. There is the danger that analysis may convert citizen participation into a sterile, technical, and bureaucratic concept. There is also, however, the danger that the concept will deteriorate into a romantic cliché that has no practical relevance.

What are needed today are analyses of citizen participation that avoid technical or romantic excess and that should describe and guide our beliefs and action. They should, to use Ludwig Wittgenstein's analogy, provide us with a "tool box" of instruments to construct meaningful theory and instruct successful practice. In this respect, analyses should generate definitions, distinctions, and descriptions that will make it easier to understand the nature of citizen participation. With such improved tools, scholars can better study and develop a body of knowledge about citizen participation; government officials can increase their capacity to plan, conduct, and evaluate citizen participation; and citizens can be clearer about values, opportunities, strategies, and tactics associated with their participation.

Although a thorough and detailed analysis of citizen participation is beyond the scope of this essay, it will address four initial and unavoidable tasks a functional analysis must consider. These tasks are the following:

1. *Defining citizen participation:* This involves providing a concrete definition that clearly identifies the essential and necessary characteristics of the term. Such a definition must be specific enough to make clear what citizen participation is and what it is not and to avoid confusing it with other things.

2. *Describing the essential elements of citizen participation:* This requires a more complete explanation of the different things characterized in a definition. It identifies more fully all the elements of the concept of citizen participation that are stated or logically implied in the definition.

3. *Determining major values of citizen participation:* This includes identifying the value assumptions that are implied in a definition, particularly in considering the historical development and use of any of the terms.

4. *Distinguishing types of citizen participation:* This involves identifying different classes or categories of citizen participation and describing the most common characteristics of each.

Defining Citizen Participation

Samuel Johnson once noted that "definitions are hazardous"; but I would add that bad definitions are worse. This is particularly true in cases of public policy, where definitions may influence how large sums of tax dollars are spent and how important institutions of a society are affected. What is most hazardous about bad definitions is not their absence or vacuousness, but rather their narrow identification of one characteristic to the exclusion of others.

Unfortunately, this has frequently been the case in the highly prescriptive literature and related policy making about citizen participation. The most noteworthy excess in this regard was the practice during the late 1960s of defining citizen participation in terms of the characteristics of citizen power and control. The problem with those definitions was that they excluded instances in which citizens participate to assist government or to carry out a valued social obligation. Today we face the opposite danger in instances where citizen participation is exclusively defined in terms of assisting and supporting administrative decision making in government to the exclusion of instances in which citizens seek to exert influence and achieve power.

What is needed, therefore, is an inclusive definition of citizen participation that clearly identifies the necessary characteristics of the concept. Perhaps the most direct way to develop such a definition is to consider the logic inherent in language by considering the etymological roots of the words *citizen* and *participation.*

Of the two words, *participation* is by far the easier to consider. *Participation* is simply derived as the past principle of the Latin *participare.* The constituent elements of this term in Latin are the noun *pars,* which means *part,* and the verb *capare,* which means *to take.* Thus, literally, the word *participation* means *to take part.*

The word *citizen* is attributable to the Anglo-French word *citizein,* which appears to be a combination of the words *cité,* meaning *city,* and *denzein,* which means *inhabitant.* The word *cité* is derived from the Latin *civitas,* which referred to a political unit (such as Rome) and to the highest political status of some inhabitants, referred to as *cives.* Therefore, *citizen* means *to be a legal inhabitant or resident of a political unit.*

On the basis of this analysis, the necessary characteristics of a definition of citizen participation appear to be as follows:

Activities, in which individuals or groups referred to as *citizens* take part;

Government as a legally defined political unit; and

Persons, referred to as *citizens,* who act as individuals or groups in relation to a unit of government.

Given these characteristics, the following analytical definition is proposed: *Citizen participation refers to purposeful activities in which people take part in relation to political units of which they are legal residents.* In so defining citizen participation, two other modifying characteristics have been added. The first is the characteristic of a *purposeful activity*; and the second is that of a *legal resident.* The reason for including these characteristic terms is that they are logically implied by other terms. The term *purposeful activity* is utilized since political units are created for useful purposes and taking part in relation to them implies a purpose on the part of the citizen or the political unit. The term *legal resident* is used because one of the implied characteristics of a political unit is the possession of laws that distinguish between legal inhabitants (citizens) and aliens. Based upon these additional distinctions, a less cumbersome definition of citizen participation might be: *Citizen participation refers to purposeful activities in which citizens take part in relation to government.*

What this definition does exclude are activities in which people participate in relation to other social institutions. Therefore, a distinction is made between citizen participation, in which people relate to the state, and social participation, in which people relate to social institutions. In making this distinction, it is not assumed that forms of social participation, such as worker participation, for example, do not have an important relationship to citizen participation. Since it appears that these forms of social participation may influence the capacity of citizens to participate in relation to government, they are referred to as related, but different, forms of participation.

The Elements of Citizen Participation

Because of the purposeful nature of citizen participation, questions of policy, planning, and evaluation become more critical as functional demands for citizen participation increase. Consequently, there is a growing practical need among policy makers, practitioners, and scholars to distinguish the elements that have to be considered in studying or advancing citizen-participation activities. The preceding analysis clearly identifies four such necessary elements:

1. *Purposes* for which citizen participation activities are undertaken;
2. *Activities* that are undertaken to achieve the purposes;
3. *Citizens* who are engaged in the activities; and
4. *Government or governmental units* in relation to which activities are undertaken.

Based upon the preceding analysis, it seems impossible to describe, plan, or evaluate adequately an instance of citizen participation without considering these elements. As noted in table 2-1, each element gives rise to a number of related questions in planning for or evaluating citizen participation.

While table 2-1 suggests important questions about these four elements of citizen participation, a few additional caveats are appropriate in regard to each.

First, it should be acknowledged that the purposes of citizen participation may be established by citizens, by government agencies, or by law. Fur-

Table 2-1
Elements of Citizen Participation

Elements	Planning Issues	Evaluative Issues
Purpose	What is to be achieved?	What was achieved and why?
	What goals are sought?	To what extent were goals met and why?
	What objectives are to be accomplished?	To what extent were objectives accomplished and why
	What specific outcomes should result?	What intended and unintended outcomes resulted and why?
Government	What is the level or levels of government to be involved in carrying out the purpose?	What levels of government were involved?
	What agencies of government, if any, have to be involved in carrying out the purpose?	In what respect was each agency of government involved?
	What policies, positions, decisions, or services will have to be effected?	In what ways and why were policies, positions, decisions, or services effected?
Citizens	Which citizens within each level of government are to participate?	What kinds of people participated and why?
	Approximately how many citizens should be involved at each level?	How many different types of people participated in different ways and why?
Activity	What activities best serve the purpose?	What activities were undertaken?
	How long should each activity last?	How long did each activity last?
	What procedures and practices will contribute to making the activity successful and cost-effective?	What practices enhanced the success of each activity? How much did the activity cost in direct and indirect per-person cost?

ther, as will be considered in the later discussion of typologies, there are four common general purposes of citizen participation. Second, there is an immense number of citizen-participation activities; and, as Judy Rosener's later essay (chapter 9) makes clear, the task of citizen-participation planning is to match appropriate methods to purpose rather than to select methods arbitrarily. Third, the types and numbers of citizens who participate in each case will vary. In general, citizen participation is geared either to all citizens, to targeted elements of the population, or to a representative group. As noted in later essays, securing the participation of minorities and the poor and establishing representative groups of citizens are two continuing problems. Fourth, contemporary government is highly diverse and complex. Therefore, citizen-participation activities may be related to legislative, administrative, and judicial branches of government. Further, citizen participation may take place at the local, county, regional, state, or national levels. In addition, the activities may be related to one or several organizational units within branches of government.

What these points make clear is that citizen participation is complex and diverse and contains infinite possibilities for variation. Nonetheless, they also demonstrate that citizen participation is susceptible to analysis according to some necessary common elements.

Normative Dimensions of Citizen Participation

This analysis has yet to make clear the important values associated with the historical development of the concept of citizenship. For example, the concept of citizenship in Roman law (*cives*) represented the highest degree of social and political status. This status was similar to the Greek concept of citizenship (*politēs*), which Aristotle described in his *Politics*. What was most distinctive about the status was that it included the conferring of such rights as holding office, jury duty, and holding property on some persons (*cives*) and not on others. By 212 A.D., with the establishment of the Constitutio Antoniniana under the emperor Caracalla, these rights of citizenship were conferred on all inhabitants of the Roman Empire. Thus, the concept of universal rights of citizenship was born.

In granting the rights of citizenship to all residents of the Roman Empire, it should not be assumed that Caracalla was motivated essentially or primarily by a commitment to rights. In truth, Rome badly needed to reduce rebellions in the provinces, increase the tax base, and strengthen the armies. Therefore, the two essential values of citizenship were demonstrated in very practical terms. Citizens were granted *rights* by the state; but in return for those rights, citizens were required to accept *obligations* to the state. Consequently, rights and obligations have developed as two of the essential values of citizenship in Western civilization.

What is particularly significant about the value of rights of citizenship in modern Western history is the extent and intensity of this value. This is particularly evident in the French and American Revolutions, with their unprecedented demands for unalienable rights, liberty, and equality. The French Declaration of the Rights of Man asserted, for example:

Law is the expression of the general will. All citizens have a right to take part, personally or by their representatives, in its formation. . . . All citizens, being equal in its eyes, are equally eligible to all public designations, places and employments, according to their capacities, and without other distinctions than those of their virtues and talents.

Significantly, following the French Revolution it became the practice to address persons as "citizen," as all other titles of status were abolished, while that of "citizen" was elevated.

The American Declaration of Independence, with its emphasis on unalienable rights, and the Bill of Rights also granted extraordinary and revolutionary rights to citizens. The Declaration of Independence went so far as to proclaim that "it is the right of the people to alter or abolish it, and to institute new government." To further ensure and protect a free and active citizenry, the Bill of Rights clearly enumerated a wide variety of rights of citizens. Making the intent of these laws even more emphatic, the Ninth Amendment declared: "The enumeration in the Constitution, of certain rights, should not be construed to deny or disparage others retained by the people."

What the history of citizenship makes clear is that important normative dimensions have accrued to it, such as rights of active and substantial participation, freedom to participate or not, obligation to participate in limited but legally stipulated activities, and equality of individual rights under law. It is for these reasons that the term *citizen participation* should be distinguished from others that are popularly used as synonyms, such as *political participation, public participation,* and *citizen involvement.*

Of these terms, *political participation* is most nearly synonymous, because it includes all the characteristics of the definition offered earlier. Thus, as descriptive-class terms, *citizen participation* and *political participation* are synonymous. What is distinctive about citizen participation is that it stresses the person rather than the state in the participatory relationsihp. Conversely, political participation stresses the state (*polis*) rather than the citizen. Accordingly, the preference for citizen participation over political participation is a normative one. In this respect, the term *citizen participation* is preferable in the Western and American context because of the values associated with the term *citizen.*

The term *public participation* is not synonymous with *citizen participation* for two reasons. First, it refers to all people included in a "public," whether or not they possess the rights and obligations of citizenship. Second, public participation can include taking part in any public institution of society or the state. Therefore, public participation includes citizen participation as well as other forms of social participation.

The term *citizen involvement* has a different connotation than *citizen participation.* The word *involve* in Latin literally is *in volvere,* which means to roll or wrap in something. What this word implies is that one thing is encumbered or controlled by another. But participation connotes variation in how things "take part" in each other, because the control may rest in either thing or may be equally shared. Citizen participation includes a variety of activities in which control may rest with either citizens or the state, or it may be equally shared. Citizen involvement can be considered as a variety of citizen participation characterized by state control of the process of participation.

Types of Citizen Participation

The previous discussion of the implied differences between citizen participation and other terms provides a basis for establishing a citizen-participation typology. The key to this typology is that citizen-participation activities are initiated and controlled by two sources, citizens and government. Therefore, we can distinguish between two general types of citizen participation: citizen-initiated and government-initiated. This distinction is frequently made when people employ the euphemisms "bottom-up" and "top-down" to describe activities.

What this distinction fails to make clear is that there are several different origins of government-initiated citizen-participation activities. Some are initiated by legislatures and administrative agencies of government for administrative purposes. Others take place periodically by law to provide continuity of leadership and to maintain stability of government. And still others include activities in which citizens are obligated by law to participate.

On the basis of these distinctions, four types or categories of citizen participation are proposed:

1. *Citizen action,* which is initiated and controlled by citizens for purposes that they determine. This category involves such activities as lobbying, public advocacy, and protest.

2. *Citizen involvement,* which is initiated and controlled by government to improve and/or to gain support for decisions, programs, or services. This category involves such activities as public hearings, consultation with advisory committees, and attitudinal surveys.

3. *Electoral participation,* which is initiated and controlled by government according to law in order to elect representatives and vote on pertinent issues. This category involves such activities as voting and working for a political candidate or in support or opposition to an issue.

4. *Obligatory participation,* which involves the mandatory responsibilities that are the legal obligations of citizenship. This category includes such activities as paying taxes, jury duty, and military service.

The more notable characteristics associated with these four categories are identified in table 2-2 according to differences in purpose, activities,

Table 2-2
Categories of Citizen Participation

	Citizen Action	Citizen Involvement	Electoral Participation	Obligatory Participation
Major distinguishing feature	Refers to activities initiated and controlled by citizens for some purpose	Refers to activities initiated and controlled by government for administrative purposes	Refers to activities to nominate and elect representatives or to vote on pertinent issues on a regularly scheduled basis established by law	Refers to activities in which participation is compulsory according to law
Major purpose	To influence decisions of government officials or voters	To improve decision making and services and develop consensus and support for decisions	To provide stability, continuity of leadership, and a workable consensus for government	To provide sufficient support for government to perform its legal functions
Examples of activities	Lobbying; public education; protest; public advocacy; civil disobedience; class-action suits	Advisory committees; public hearings; goals programs; surveys; hot lines; volunteer programs	Voting; running for office; working for a candidate; volunteering to help a political party	Paying taxes; doing military service; jury duty
Dominant concerns	Organizing effectively; obtaining appropriate information; developing support; raising funds; making maximum political and public impact	Involving more citizens; informing citizens better; broadening the range of citizen representation; maintaining citizen interest; effective utilization of citizen involvement in decision making; obtaining necessary funds	Increasing voter turnout; raising funds for a party or candidate	Increasing public understanding of the obligations of citizenship; attracting and retaining capable jurors and military personnel
Typically interested groups	Neighborhood and community action groups; public-interest and consumer groups; community agencies; individual citizens	Legislative committees; administrative agencies; regulatory agencies	Elected officials; political parties; political candidates	Judges; court officers; military leaders; tax officials

dominant concerns, and groups that typically are involved with each. This typology illustrates why citizen participation means different things to different people. In practice, citizen participation may mean four different forms of activity, each of which has its distinct tradition, agenda, style, language, and following.

As there are distinctive categories of citizen participation, there are also appropriate distinctions to be made within each category. For example, within the category of citizen action, there are distinctions to be made among activities initiated by grassroots groups, public-interest groups, special-interest groups, and individuals. In the case of citizen involvement, distinctions can be made in terms of activities initiated by the executive branch, the legislative branch, or independently by a government agency. Although opportunities for electoral participation are established by law, candidates may be nominated through the initiatives of political parties, special groups, or the individuals themselves. Referenda items can be initiated by legislative bodies or by citizens.

Because of the different purposes among the categories of citizen participation, it is not surprising to find that those who are strongly committed to the categories of citizen action, citizen involvement, and electoral participation frequently question the value of the other categories. For example, citizen activists often are suspicious of the motives in citizen-involvement programs of government agencies and the possibility of being co-opted; government officials may fear that aggressive citizen action is unrealistic or is not representative of the majority of citizens; and many politicians and democratic theorists who are predominantly committed to electoral participation may warn that increased citizen action and citizen involvement will make government unmanageable and will undermine stability. It is not uncommon to find that the term *citizen participation* is used by many advocates of these three positions as a negative term to identify another position that they fear. However, there are many instances in which advocates of citizen action, citizen involvement, or electoral participation employ the term *citizen participation* to indicate the type of participation to which they are committed. Thus, *citizen participation* is frequently used as a normative term designating a type of participation that people are for or against.

By defining, describing essential elements, determining major values, and distinguishing different types, a modest attempt has been made in this essay to establish a framework for a clearer understanding of the phenomenon of citizen participation. This discussion has not assumed that it is an appropriate end in itself, nor has it considered the question of the appropriate limits of citizen participation. What the essay is intended to offer are some distinctions and interpretations that may facilitate investigation of such questions as these as well as other critical questions of theory, research, and practice. In this sense, it has sought to demonstrate that citizen participation is not immune from thoughtful and systematic analysis. Although such analysis is difficult and is resisted by inherent dilemmas, that is all the more reason to encourage rather than to avoid the task.

Notes

1. Hans Spiegel and Stephen Mittenthal, "The Many Faces of Citizen Participation: A Bibliographic Overview," *Citizen Participation in Urban Development,* Vol. I. (Washington: National Training Laboratories, 1968), pp. 3-7.

2. Charles L. Stevenson, *Ethics and Language* (New Haven: Yale University Press, 1949).

3. Ernst Cassirer, *Language and Myth* (New York: Dover Books, 1946).

3

What Do We Know about Citizen Participation? A Selective Review of Research

Barry Checkoway and Jon Van Til

Introduction

The best research is art, craft, and science—but first of all it is art, based on the ability to listen and to understand.

As artist, the researcher listens, watches, and tries to understand the worlds of those persons and institutions being studied; as craftsperson, the researcher seeks to put into an overall pattern the various fragments of reality as perceived by those whose lives are studied; as scientist, the researcher ties the findings from one research situation into an overarching set of assumptions and tested propositions that is the accepted consensus of researchers as to what is known in a specific field at a specific point in time.

Research on citizen participation has been characterized by differences and controversies about even the most fundamental phenomena in the field. Ask the experts, "What is citizen participation?" and no two of them will agree. To one or another researcher, citizen participation can refer to a public relations program to build support for agency plans; or to the deliberations of those who hold positions on a city-wide advisory committee; or to acts of voting for political representatives; or to a transfer of power from central government to local territorial or functional units; or to an organized effort to engage in protest or some form of direct action. All appear under the general rubric of citizen participation. The pattern is one in which research findings are fragmented across a variety of professional disciplines among which there are few shared meanings and methodologies. It is not surprising that two observers would conclude: "Citizen participation virtually defies generalization and delights in reducing abstractions to dust."[1]

What is needed is to identify the general propositions from the research literature on citizen participation and to inventory the state of knowledge in the field. Citizen participation is a field of knowledge, but not an academic discipline. As David Popenoe notes, the primary task of a discipline is to organize and analyze a variety of concrete phenomena from an accepted point of view. "The primary task of a field, on the other hand, is to focus a variety of such analytic disciplines on one set of concrete phenomena,'' he continues. A constraint on the development of participation is not that it is interdisciplinary but that its general propositions require organization.[2] Science grows through differences and controversies, but it begins with only relative consensus. A field can only go forward when its researchers know which way they are facing. At this early point in the history of citizen participation, what is needed is some organization of knowledge in the field.

The purpose of this chapter is to review the present state of knowledge about citizen participation. Our aim is not to summarize, or even to mention, all the significant research on citizen participation that has been conducted, for a comprehensive bibliography on the subject, listing published materials alone, could easily run twice as long as this chapter.[3] Rather, we want to highlight a number of research studies that we view as exemplary, to draw from them the general propositions that represent the major areas of agreement among researchers, and to indicate unanswered or remaining questions in the field. They are not the only propositions or questions about citizen participation, but they are among the most important.

We begin, then, with our own process of research craftsmanship, sorting through the hundreds of published studies of citizen participation (and some unpublished, for the network of reseachers also involves informal contact among them) written by sociologists, political scientists, planners, community activists, social workers, and representatives of many other disciplines and professions. As we review this literature, we are struck by the variety of its methodologies and approaches, as in the following:

1. A study of two antipornography campaigns in the 1960s, one in the South and one in the Midwest, which finds that the quest for personal status by lower-middle-class, largely white, Protestant participants explains their determined efforts to preserve threatened societal values.[4]
2. A study of 53 ''challenging organizations'' that arose in American society between 1800 and 1945, which finds that social movements are not greatly different from politics as usual, but are simply another way of advancing a concern for social and personal change.[5]
3. A study of three groups of welfare recipients in an Eastern metropolitan setting in the late 1960s, which finds that the most serious barriers limiting full citizen participation by the poor are those of confronting official ''nondecisions'' that sought to ignore their concerns, maintaining group cohesion, and raising and developing resources in the face of heavy drains on their own time and energy.[6]
4. A study of the types of citizen-participation programs developed in 227 cities as federally supported community action programs in the 1960s, which finds that citizen participation can improve the quality of service-

delivery, increase citizen trust, and advance the process of self-government.[7]

5. A review of one man's experiences and approaches in seeking to facilitate direct action by citizens' groups in their own interest, which concludes that there is a set of "rules for radicals" that can guide their effective action.[8]

Let us turn to what this literature shows. What do we know about citizen participation? And what unsolved problems remain to be the focus of continuing research in this field?

What Do We Know about Citizen Participation: Some Propositions Substantiated by Research

1. Participation Is Central to the Functioning of a Democratic Society. The question "Does organized citizen participation enhance the development of democracy?" receives an almost instinctive answer: "Of course it does!" To be sure, political and social theorists of every major democratic stripe—liberal, conservative, and radical—have found citizen participation to play an important role in the development of full democracy.

Kasperson and Breitbart, in their excellent review of the literature, *Participation, Decentralization, and Advocacy Planning,*[9] examine the orientation of three traditions they identify as elitist, Marxist, and citizen theorist. The elitists[10] warn of the dangers of excess participation but see a central role for citizen participation. They are concerned that participation by those who are not fully informed or able may "overheat" decision-making structures and detract from the overall quality of public policy decisions. Such thinkers do, however, see a central role for participation by the electorate and by those sectors of the citizenry that are fully informed. The Marxists[11] tend to argue that participation within captalism that is not aimed at the building of socialism is a sham. They call for a participation that is egalitarian, liberating, conscious, and related to class objectives. Thus, contemporary Marxists throw their support to "local action, not citizen participation," and urge those who support the "ideology of participationism" to realize that what they call " 'citizen control', without other fundamental changes in the political and economic system, . . . results [in] . . . the reintegration of marginal elements and the bolstering of the status quo."[12] Citizen theorists[13] draw on a long tradition of liberal and pluralist thought that views participation as a crucial educative experience for the citizen and an open-ended process of revitalization for the society. These theorists see a long-range drift toward equality in a society in which full participation exists, rejecting the Marxist faith in revolutionary transformation and the elitists' belief in an unchanging human nature.

How one views the world through ideological perspectives—elitist, Marxist, or citizen theorist—directly affects how one evaluates any particular participatory experience. But the important point for now is that each tradition values participation in one form or another and finds that it contributes to the vision of democracy. Not surprisingly each finds forms of participation to approve and disapprove in contemporary society, which takes us to our second point.

2. Participation Is Exercised in Differential Frequency by Individuals and Groups in Society. Studies of the scope of participation in America indicate that a significant proportion of the population engages in little or no participation and that small groups are extremely active.[14] V.O. Key has likened the pattern of participation to a layer cake in which the thinnest layer is made up of the most active participants.[15] Thompson cites evidence to confirm that only about 4 percent to 5 percent of Americans are active in political parties or campaigns and that turnout in elections at all levels is low.[16] Milbrath concludes that about one-third of the population is apathetic or passive; that another 60 percent play spectator roles; and that only 5 percent to 7 percent are "gladiators" who attend meetings and actively participate.[17]

Those few individuals who do actively participate are not representative of the population overall. "One of the most thoroughly substantiated propositions in all of social science is that persons near the center of society are more likely to participate in politics than persons near the periphery," according to Milbrath.[18] Income, education, and occupational status all correlate positively with individual participation and contribute to personal characteristics and social attitudes that support further activity. Higher status individuals participate out of proportion to their numbers. Organized participants also "reflect an upper-class tendency."[19] Several studies have documented the dominance of organized economic interests and "blue ribbon" citizens in federal domestic programs,[20] and of "local notables" and the "socially elite" in local voluntary associations, on citizen advisory councils, and even on community poverty boards.[21]

Although an active social science debate continues over whether or not public decisions are dominated by some monolithic elite or by rival elites, there remains agreement that the most active participants are few in number and unrepresentative of the population overall. According to Schattschneider, "the flaw in the pluralist heaven is that the heavenly chorus sings with a strong upper-class accent."[22]

3. Low-Income Citizens Participate Less Than Those in Higher Socioeconomic Categories, but Many of Them Do Participate Actively. This proposition generally holds true whether one uses level of income, education, or occupation as a measure of social status.[23] The indication is that most poor people are less likely than higher status people to join organizations, vote, attend political meetings, and participate in public affairs. Studies show that blacks continue to be underrepresented among the participants in society, although it is becoming increasingly clear that this fact is almost entirely explained by the socioeconomic distress that so often accompanies being black.[24] Low-income and minority citizens often participate less in government programs, even when these programs are presumably designed to elicit their participation.[25] The explanation for this is in dispute. Some analysts attribute it to institutional bias and discriminatory practices;[26] others attribute it to the political ethos and subcultural pathology of the citizens themselves.[27] Whatever the explanation, the fact of differential participation remains.

This is not to suggest that low-income and minority citizens do not participate at all or are without influence in public decisions and policy outcomes. On the contrary, although their overall participation is relatively less than that of others who are closer to the center of the fabric of American society, there is evidence among them of long-term increases in political self-awareness and efficacy,[28] and of organized action groups employing skillful leaders and organizational tactics that increase their influence and win rewards.[29]

4. Groups That Do Participate Can Surmount Barriers to their Participation, but the Gaining of Access May Not Be Easy. Participation is not universal: some people participate, others do not. Some participate with great effect and impact; others find only frustration and failure for their efforts. Further, some people choose not to participate: they have other things to do with the scarce resources of time and energy; or they simply do not believe that participation will be worth the effort.

Bachrach and Baratz have written of the "mobilization of bias" that is involved in participation.[30] By this they mean that interests that are supported by organizations are more likely to be successful than those that are unorganized. In a study of three groups of welfare recipients in the process of seeking to organize to represent their interests, Van Til tested for the strength of seven possible barriers to their effective action.[31] Of these barriers, three were found to be most serious: (1) cohesion and integration—the degree to which the groups' members were able to work together; (2) raising resources for the group—the degree to which the group was able to raise funds, cooperate with other groups, and be provided with the necessary technical assistance in the form of community organizers, and the like; and (3) community and institutional nondecisions—the degree to which institutions and agencies in society refused to recognize the seriousness of the demands brought by the groups.

Van Til concluded from his study that the very process of access to the decision-making process was problematic for these groups of welfare recipients. Once they were organized and recognized, their concerns were listened to and acted upon. But until they established their presence, they were ignored, abused, and generally rendered ineffective by the officials they sought to influence. Van Til concluded that the method of direct action (for example, sitting in the offices of officials who ignored them) was the single most effective means of eliminating the mobilization of bias that blocked the groups access to the arena of group decision making.[32]

5. There Is an Ever-Present Force of "Potential Participation" in Every Major Institution. Citizen participation is almost never fully mobilized; there is always another group, individual, or action that can be brought into play. The result is that potential participation is also an important factor to take into account in assessing the impact of citizen participation. To the elitist, the presence of potential participation indicates a flexible situation in which there is room for both maneuver and compromise—and in which the costs of full mobilization of all participants need not be paid.[33] To the citizen theorist, too much potential participation means a lack of involvement and excessive apathy. Whatever the assessment, the value of potential participation is nonetheless acknowledged.[34]

Zurcher and Kirkpatrick, in their study of the careers of two antipornography movements, clearly illustrate how potential participation develops and is used by citizen-participation leaders.[35] They find that participants in the antipornography movement were less likely to have engaged in political activity, or to have expressed an interest in politics, than the persons who took participatory roles in opposition to the banning of pornography.

Leaders of citizen-participation activities often use indicators of potential participation to indicate the strength of their organizations. Leaders of the Alliance for Volunteerism, for example, a national coalition organization of 19 associations, sometimes refer to their access to six million volunteers, themselves related to the member organizations in some way, although an overwhelming proportion of these volunteers are entirely unaware of their link to the Alliance. It is less clear what claim the six million can make on the national organization; such are the ambiguities of potential participation.

6. "Full Participation" Does Not Necessarily Constitute a Progressive Force, but Rather Includes the Mobilization of Forces from both Right and Left. It is sometimes assumed that citizen participation, if fully mobilized, would usher in an overwhelming demand for progressive changes in power and policy. This assumption is vigorously resisted by elitists, who note that among the nonparticipants are many individuals and interests not inclined to support either progressive or democratic change.[36]

Increasingly, radical theorists have tended to accept the plausibility of the same conclusion. Thus, Parenti identifies as a potential direction for change:

Mass discontent may be mobilized but in a rightward direction, one that accepts the corporate system and the hierarchical society and concentrates on nonclass issues, built upon the fears and anxieties provoked by military defeats abroad, economic recession at home, and the weakening of authority and decline of traditional cultural and ideological institutions. Today, one can see early signs of such a rightist protest, focusing on issues like the abolition of legal abortion, school busing, opposition to equal-rights laws for women, gays, and minorities, restoration of the death penalty, and the antiunion "right to work" laws. Rightists from the John Birch Society have begun to link these immediate issues to their own virulent anticommunism, racism, and militarism. Support is drawn mostly from the newly rich, small business people, and lower-middle class elements, and growing incursions are being made among the working class.[37]

The field research of Zurcher and Kirkpatrick dramatically illustrates the power of right-wing citizen participation. They conclude their study of antipornography movements by noting:

So long as social change impinges upon the prestige and power of a central life style in American society as presently structured, it is likely that there will be symbolic crusades in service of that prestige, power, and centrality. The Supreme Court's recent emphasis on local community standards for the determination of what is pornographic may be a dramatic precedent, facilitating the expression of status discontent and escalating the possibilities for symbolic crusades. If there can be a determination of the dominant local standards for pornography, why not for marijuana use, abortion, homosexuality, and so on? Why not for the dominant local life style? The Supreme Court may have made symbolic crusades a more important part of American society than ever.[38]

7. Organized Participation Is Internally a Differentiating Force, in Which Leaders and Followers Emerge, Issues Develop, and Contrasting Interests May Come into Conflict and Proliferate. This finding is among the oldest and best established in the research literature on citizen participation. It was most dramatically stated by Robert Michels in the phrase "Who says organization, says oligarchy." Michels' research showed that organization provided powers and gains to leaders that made them unaccountable to their followers—and that power itself breeds more power.[39]

Michels' findings have been dramatically confirmed by several recent studies of citizen participation in poverty communities. Brill, in a study of a failed rent strike, focuses on the way in which one of the group's organizers consistently acted to advance his own, rather than his group's interests. The organizer engaged in a series of sexual encounters with the striking tenants, which served to discourage attendance at the tenants' regular meetings. "In working to keep the tenants on strike, he persistently withheld information, distorted and fabricated facts, and instilled fear."[40] Fellow organizers did little to intervene, following a "mutual noninterference" policy, and they shared a lack of respect for the women tenants who were their basic constituency. Kramer, in his comparative case study of participation in community action programs, comes to conclusions which, while less dramatic than Brill's, also support Michels:

Those (of the poor) who were employed in the CAP gained experience and skills and many of the CAP participants improved their ur.derstanding, but there was widespread recognition among both groups in all communities that the hard-core and unaffiliated poor had really not been reached, nor did they benefit in any substantial way from the programs and services of the war on poverty.[41]

To be sure, a creative organization can take steps to prevent its organizers from leading it to failure by advancing their own interests solely. A growing literature of sensible, seasoned advice on leadership in community organizations is available and should be consulted.[42] Every organization must build in the structures necessary to provide feedback and accountability to its leaders—for only by such self-consciousness of its own process can the negative aspects of the iron law of oligarchy be thwarted and responsible leadership assured.

8. Administrative Agencies Often Use Participation As an Instrument to Achieve Their Own Ends without Any Significant Transfer of Power. Recent years have witnessed an increase in the number of official participation programs employed by administrative agencies. In the last eight years alone, there have been more than 25 hearings in Congress focusing on the need for greater public participation in federal agency proceedings, and participation has now become part of every major federal domestic program. City governments have put into practice a wide range of participation structures, and the outpouring of citizen-complaint bureaus, little city halls, and citizen advisory committees, to cite only a few examples, has been impressive indeed.[43] Methods to improve communications among agency administrators and citizens have been especially numerous.[44]

Most of the official methods adopted are used to achieve administrative or institutional ends. Participation is intended to satisfy minimum legal requirements set by federal programs, or to provide public-relations activity and build support for agency plans, or to diffuse antagonism and reduce hostile confrontations with citizens, or to legitimate decisions made elsewhere.[45] The pattern is one in which administrative agencies favor participation that is not disruptive of program management and oppose participation that results in citizen control over key aspects of programs.[46] Administrative agencies thus place heavy reliance on "safe" methods, such as public hearings, that keep participation under careful control and rarely allow genuine "decentralization," which would transfer power to local territorial or functional units.[47] Thus, it is not surprising that several studies have documented the failures of official participation programs to transfer power.

9. There Are Strong Administrative Obstacles to the Expansion of Participation in American Society. Some of these obstacles are institutional or administrative in nature. Administrative agencies place an emphasis on precise measurement and technical rationality and seek to overcome disorganization, haphazardness, and amateurism in program management. The administrative values of efficiency, economy, and control are central throughout.[48] Citizen participation is often seen as the antithesis of these values. Citizens are perceived to lack information and professional expertise, to hold views that are difficult to quantify, and to create problems for administrators and managers. Their participation is expected to cause long delays in action, to expand the number and intensity of conflicts, and to increase the cost of operations. It is not surprising that one agency administrator would declare: "I share enthusiasm for maximum feasible participation in the process of local governments, but I also favor orderly administrative processes and governmental action not unduly impeded by neighborhood struggles and competing squabbles . . ."; and that another could state: "From a bureaucrat's viewpoint, there is always trouble in citizen organizations."[49]

In addition, administrative agencies are often influenced by those with an economic interest in limiting participation. A recent congressional study found that regulated industries commonly comprise 90 percent of presentations in federal regulatory agency proceedings and that agency decisions also commonly reflect their views.[50] These industries are also active in constraining the participation of citizen organizations. The issue is not that agencies are necessarily partisan or are captured by the industries they regulate, but rather that agency officials depend greatly upon outside sources of information and support and respond to the most powerful inputs they receive.

10. Organization Is a Central Factor for Citizens Seeking to Participate. Americans traditionally have structured their participation through formal organizations and voluntary associations. These organizations serve two major functions. One function is to mobilize individual citizen attitudes and develop a common program. Organizational involvement can stimulate awareness of common problems, increase levels of citizen efficacy and activity,[51] and provide a context in which to reach agreement and build a sense of collective identity around which a program can be developed. Another function is to generate power to fulfill the program that is developed. Organizations can enhance the ability of individual citizens to exercise influence and control. The assumption is that citizen participation cannot be considered apart from a context of politics and that individual citizens wield more authentic power when combined together in organizations.[52]

Citizen organizations have increased in number and capacity in recent years.[53] The contemporary movement is said to have originated with the organized protests of minorities and then to have spread throughout the society. As a result, the once-held image of Americans as spectators or apathetics has given way under a virtual stampede of civil-rights movements, public-action councils, consumer coalitions, neighborhood associations, and other citizen organizations independent of government. Some of these organizations employ full-time professional organizers with knowledge of organizational tactics that can win rewards. Although these organizers are sometimes perceived by agency administrators as exceptional or irresponsible, the evidence is that they strongly embrace democratic values, are well integrated into the community, and employ tactics similar to those used by agency officials themselves.[54] These organizations have begun to have a significant impact on administrative agencies and public decisions.[55]

Unresolved or Open Questions about Citizen Participation

We conclude our review of research on citizen participation by examining five important questions we cannot answer from our examination of available research.

1. What Institutional Methods or Structures for Participation Are in Use? In the governmental and administrative rush to citizen participation, there has been no comprehensive effort to inventory the great number of methods in use. Several typologies categorize selected methods according to the value orientations and conceptual frameworks of the authors, but make no attempt to assess the field overall.[56] An excellent agency catalogue describes 37 current or emergent methods, but gives little indication of the scope or effectiveness of each.[57] A 1972 publication of the Advisory Commission on Intergovernmental Relations reports on a survey of all cities and counties of over 25,000 population to determine the extent to which local governments employed participation methods. Not surveyed is the wide range of structures at other levels of government or on the unofficial neighborhood scale.[58] In order to achieve a really complete understanding of citizen participation, researchers must now undertake a more comprehensive accounting of practice in the field. Indeed, only by such studies can the status of the participation field overall begin to be known.

2. In What Ways Does Participation Make a Difference in the Decisions and Policy Outcomes of Government, and What Kind of Difference? It is remarkable how little research and analysis have been done on the quality of participation practice. Previous studies have focused on the desirability of participation, or on the right or competence of citizens to participate, or on aggregate trends in national participation, or on past participation practice once the fundamental principles are embraced. Much has been written on the ideology of participation. Indeed, so common is the focus on ideology that there has resulted a tendency to rely upon it as an accurate description of practice. But participation is not simply a body of concepts, a manner of thinking, or a set of theories and aims. It is also a practical activity in which people engage and which itself is subject to analysis. Yet the study of participation practice is neither well-researched nor in serious question. Does participation work? Does it make government more responsive? Does it improve the delivery system? Few major studies address these questions and the important issues they raise.

Those few studies that do examine participation practice tend to take the stated aims for granted and to evaluate particular methods in terms of their frequency and number. Thus it is common to claim that because a participation method aims to "involve" citizens, and because proceedings are held and people attend and express views, participation must necessarily have taken place. Evidence indicates, however, that an extensive gap may separate stated participation aims and actual practice, and that the number of proceedings held or the number of people who take part in them is not an adequate measure of their quality. Although most analytic discussion centers on the scope of participation, quality is its most important attribute. Participation quality is effective if it influences a particular decision or produces a favorable policy outcome.[59] But few studies approach participation as a practice, and little is known about the quality of even the major methods employed.

Since most government or administrative agencies currently use and will continue to use participation methods, it is long past time to assess what is known about how or whether they work. Indeed, it would seem the most elementary form of intelligent administration and responsible citizenship to assess the quality of so major a movement.

3. Would a Society in Which Full Participation Was the Practice Be a Utopia in Which Interests Were Clearly Articulated and Met, or a Distopia of Static and Stalemate in Which Interests Would Clash in a Heated-Up En-

vironment? We have noted that full participation in American society implies the activation of many interests and groups that would advocate rightist, as well as leftist, solutions to problems. What would society be like if all these "sleeping dogs" awoke and began to prowl about with the rest of us?

We don't find the answer to this question in the research literature, which is not surprising, because such full mobilization has never been realized in our society. Nonetheless, we do note that the issue has been joined by two schools of liberal thought—the pluralists and the idealists. The pluralists differ among themselves as to the amount of participation any system can reasonably accommodate. One group among them, the minimalists,[60] contends that the system will easily become overheated and that pluralism can only work if many interests remain inactive, at least at any one point in time. The other group, the maximalists,[61] tends to greater optimism about the amount of pluralism that can be accommodated productively in a system.

Idealist thinkers, on the other hand, place a greater value on one kind of participation, direct political participation, above all others. They argue that only from the quality of dialogue and decision uniquely engendered by the political system can full participation, without exhaustion, be achieved. As latter-day followers of Plato, this group is skeptical about the impact of many forms of specialized citizen participation, and urges the development, rather, of a broader conception of citizenship.[62]

4. What Role Does Participation Play in the Development and Maintenance of a Just and Productive Social Democracy? The real question is: Is participation enough? Or, do we need to assure that the "right kind" of participation is especially nurtured and fostered? Once again, students of citizen participation are predisposed to differ with one another on ideological grounds. Idealists and Marxists are inclined to insist on the "proper forms" of participation; pluralists and elitists are more inclined to let a thousand participatory flowers bloom and find in their contention the seeds of full democratic process.

The answer to this question can be illuminated by research. There is already a debate among historians over whether participation in the earliest stages of community building enhances the formation of democracy.[63] There also are a number of relatively self-contained communities, such as Isla Vista near the University of California at Santa Barbara, or Crested Butte in Colorado, where either a homogeneity of participatory-oriented population or a common threat to the survival of the community give rise to conditions of high participation and potential community change. Tracing the impact of such a process would illuminate our knowledge of the consequences for social justice and the creation of democratic structures that attach to augmented citizen participation.

5. What Is the Appropriate Role for the Participation Professional? In the clamor and controversy of the early 1960s, the participation professional was generally characterized as an advocate who openly recommended particular group interests in society.[64] Emphasis was placed on providing technical assistance to the poor, the black, and others customarily excluded from planning and public affairs. Scarcely a day passed when the media failed to report some action by advocates to aid or organize citizen clients against construction of a metropolitan expressway, federal intervention in urban renewal, or expansion of a university or hospital into nearby areas.[65]

Since that time, the advocacy role of the participation professional has been challenged. Some critics view advocacy as a new form of coercion, in which advocates impose personal values on citizens and excluded them from the planning process.[66] Others view advocacy as a new form of co-optation, which diverts the powerless from organizational tactics that are more effective in winning rewards.[67] Others view advocacy as stopping short of radical self-awareness, in which citizens would develop the competence to plan and advocate meaningfully for themselves.[68] Even the original advocates came to reformulate their position.[69] And agency administrators throughout view advocacy as a threat to administrative values and have sought a more technical or administrative approach to the field.[70]

The search for an appropriate role for the participation professional is like that for the meaning of participation itself. Each derives from a body of theories and values that define basic ends. None is agreed to by all practitioners, just as no one theory is accepted by all. We do not expect this issue to be resolved within our open and multifaceted society. But we do anticipate a great deal of participation in the development and playing of the roles of participation professionals, participation researchers, and participants themselves.

Notes

1. Hans B.C. Spiegel and Stephen D. Mittenthal, "The Many Faces of Citizen Participation," *Citizen Participation in Urban Development* (Washington: National Training Laboratories Institute for Applied Behavioral Science, 1968), p. 3.

2. Other efforts to identify the general propositions about citizen participation include: Lester W. Milbrath, *Political Participation* (Chicago: Rand McNally, 1965); Judith V. May, *Citizen Participation: A Review of the Literature* (Monticello, Ill.: Council of Planning Librarians Exchange Bibliography No. 210-211, 1971); Hans B.C. Spiegel, "Citizen Participation in Federal Programs: A Review," *Journal of Voluntary Action Research,* Monograph No. 1 (1971), pp. 4-31, reprinted in Roland L. Warren, ed., *Perspectives on the American Community* (Chicago: Rand McNal-

ly, 1973), pp. 365-389; and Roger E. Kasperson and Myrna Brietbart, *Participation, Decentralization, and Advocacy Planning* (Washington: Association of American Geographers, 1974); Popenoe, "On the Meaning of 'Urban' in Urban Studies," *Urban Affairs Quarterly* 1 (1963).

3. Barry Checkoway et al., *Citizen Participation Technology* (Monticello, Ill.: Council of Planning Librarians Exchange Bibliography No. 1329, 1977).

4. Louis A. Zurcher, Jr., and R. George Kirkpatrick, *Citizens for Decency: Anti-Pornography Crusaders as Status Defense* (Austin: University of Texas Press, 1976).

5. William A. Gamson, *The Strategy of Social Protest* (Homewood, Ill.: The Dorsey Press, 1975).

6. Jon Van Til, "Becoming Participants: Dynamics of Access Among the Welfare Poor," *Social Science Quarterly* 54 (1973):345-358.

7. Richard L. Cole, *Citizen Participation and the Urban Policy Process* (Lexington, Mass.: Lexington Books, D.C. Heath and Company, 1974).

8. Saul D. Alinsky, *Rules for Radicals* (New York: Random House, 1971).

9. Kasperson and Brietbart, *Participation*.

10. V.O. Key, Jr., *Public Opinion and American Democracy* (New York: Knopf, 1961); Gabriel A. Almond and Sidney Verba, *The Civic Culture* (Boston: Little, Brown, 1965); and James Q. Wilson and Edward C. Banfield, "Public Regardingness as a Value Premise in Voting Behavior," *American Political Science Review* 58 (1964):876-887.

11. Paulo Friere, *Pedagogy of the Oppressed* (New York: Herder and Herder, 1970); and Michael Evans, "Karl Marx and the Concept of Political Participation," in Geraint Parry, ed., *Participation in Politics* (Manchester, England: Manchester University Press, 1972), pp. 127-150.

12. Katharine Colt, "Local Action, Not Citizen Participation," in William K. Tabb and Larry Sawers, eds., *Marxism and the Metropolis* (New York: Oxford University Press, 1978), pp. 297-311.

13. Carl J. Friedrich, *The New Belief in the Common Man* (Boston: Little, Brown, 1942); and Robert J. Pranger, *The Eclipse of Citizenship: Power and Participation in Contemporary Society* (New York: Holt, Rinehart and Winston, 1968).

14. Mibrath, *Political Participation*; Kasperson and Brietbart, *Participation*; Robert E. Lane, *Political Life: Why and How People Get Involved in Politics* (New York: The Free Press, 1959); Angus Campbell et al., *The American Voter* (New York: Wiley, 1960); and Sidney Verba and Norman H. Nie, *Participation in America: Political Democracy and Social Equality* (New York: Harper and Row, 1972).

15. Key, *Public Opinion*.

16. Dennis F. Thompson, *The Democratic Citizen* (Cambridge, England: Cambridge University Press, 1970).

17. Milbrath, *Political Participation.*

18. Ibid., p. 113.

19. E.E. Schattschneider, *The Semisovereign People* (Hinsdale, Ill.: Dryden Press, 1960), p. 33.

20. "Citizen Participation in Urban Renewal," *Columbia Law Review* 66 (1966):485-607; Lillian Rubin, "Maximum Feasible Participation: The Origins, Implications and Present Status," *Poverty and Human Resources Abstracts* 2 (1967):5-18; Paul Peterson, "Forms of Representation: Participation of the Poor in Community Action Programs," *American Political Science Review* 64 (1970):491-507; James Lorimer, *A Citizen's Guide to City Politics* (Toronto: James Lewis and Samuel, 1972); and John H. Mollenkopf, "The Post-War Politics of Urban Development," *Politics and Society* (1975), pp. 247-495.

21. Sherry Arnstein, "A Ladder of Citizen Participation," *Journal of the American Institute of Planners* 35 (1969):216-224; Sherry Arnstein for the North City Areawide Council, "Maximum Feasible Manipulation," *City* (1970), pp. 30-38; and Douglas Yates, *Neighborhood Democracy* (Lexington, Mass.: Lexington Books, D.C. Heath and Company, 1973).

22. Schattschneider, *The Semisovereign People,* p. 35.

23. Milbrath, *Political Participation*; and Verba and Nie, *Participation in America.*

24. Thompson, *The Democratic Citizen*; and Bruce London, "Racial Differences in Social and Political Participation: It's Not Simply a Matter of Black and White," *Social Science Quarterly* 56 (1975):274-286.

25. Herbert J. Gans, *The Urban Villagers: Group and Class in the Life of Italian-Americans* (New York: The Free Press, 1962); Martin Anderson, *The Federal Bulldozer* (Cambridge, Mass.: M.I.T. Press, 1964); and Barry Checkoway, "The Failure of Citizen Participation in Federal Housing Programs," *Planning & Public Policy* 3 (1977):1-4.

26. Alan A. Altshuler, *Community Control: The Black Demand for Participation in Large American Cities* (New York: The Bobbs-Merrill Company, 1970).

27. James Q. Wilson, "Planning and Politics: Citizen Participation in Urban Renewal," *Journal of the American Institute of Planners* 29 (1963):242-249.

28. Verba and Nie, *Participation in America.*

29. Stokely Carmichael and Charles V. Hamilton, *Black Power* (New York: Vintage Books, 1967); Daniel Bell and Virginia Held, "The Community Revolution," *The Public Interest* 16 (1969):142-177; Frances Fox Piven and Richard Cloward, *Regulating the Poor: The Functions of Public Welfare* (New York: Pantheon Books, 1971); Susan S. Fainstein and Norman I. Fainstein, eds., *The View from Below: Urban Politics and Social Policy* (Boston: Little, Brown, 1972); Curt Lamb, *Political Power in Poor*

Neighborhoods (Cambridge, Mass.: Schenkman Publishing Company, 1975); and Janice E. Perlman, "Grassrooting the System," *Social Policy* 7 (1976):4-20.

30. Peter Bachrach and Morton S. Baratz, *Power and Poverty* (New York: Oxford University Press, 1970).

31. Van Til, "Becoming Participants."

32. Similar conclusions have been reached by Piven and Cloward, *Regulating the Poor,* Michael Parenti, "Power and Pluralism: A View from the Bottom," *The Journal of Politics* 32 (1970):501-530.

33. Bernard R. Berelson, Paul Lazarsfeld, and William McPhee, *Voting: A Study of Opinion Formation in a Presidential Campaign* (Chicago: University of Chicago Press, 1954).

34. T.B. Bottomore, *Elites and Society* (New York: Basic Books, 1964).

35. Zurcher and Kirkpatrick, *Citizens for Decency.*

36. Seymour Martin Lipset, *Political Man* (New York: Doubleday, 1960).

37. Michael Parenti, *Power and the Powerless* (New York: St. Martin's Press, 1978), p. 228.

38. Zurcher and Kirkpatrick, *Citizens for Decency,* pp. 347-348.

39. Robert Michels, *Political Parties* (Glencoe, Ill.: The Free Press, 1958).

40. Harry Brill, *Why Organizers Fail* (Berkeley: University of California Press, 1971), p. 154.

41. Ralph M. Kramer, *Participation of the Poor: Comparative Community Case Studies in the War on Poverty* (Englewood Cliffs, N.J.: Prentice-Hall, 1969), p. 256.

42. Alinsky, *Rules for Radicals*; Ronald Lippitt and Eva Schindler-Rainman, *The Volunteer Community* (Washington: National Training Laboratories Institute for Applied Social Science, 1971); Michael Walzer, *Political Action: A Practical Guide to Movement Politics* (Chicago: Quadrangle, 1971), George Brager and Harry Specht, *Community Organizing* (New York: Columbia University Press, 1973); and Fred M. Cox, John L. Erlich, Jack Rothman, and John E. Tropman, eds., *Tactics and Techniques of Community Practice* (Itasca, Ill.: F.E. Peacock, 1977).

43. Advisory Commission on Intergovernmental Relations, *The New Grass Roots Government?* (Washington: Advisory Committee on Intergovernmental Relations, 1972); Robert K. Yin et al., *Citizen Organizations: Increasing Client Control over Services* (Santa Monica: Rand Corporation, 1973); and U.S. Department of Transportation, *Effective Citizen Participation in Transportation Planning* (Washington: U.S. Department of Transportation, 1976).

44. Advisory Commission on Intergovernmental Relations, *The New*

Grass Roots Government; and Henry Schmandt, "Decentralization: A Structural Imperative," in George Frederickson, ed., *Neighborhood Control in the 1970's: Politics, Administration, and Citizen Participation* (New York: Chandler Publishing Company, 1973), pp. 17-35.

45. Arnstein, "A Ladder of Citizen Participation"; and Barry Checkoway, "The Politics of Public Hearings" (manuscript in preparation).

46. Speigel, "Citizen Participation in Federal Programs," p. 368.

47. Kasperson and Brietbart, *Participation*.

48. Spiegel, "Citizen Participation in Federal Programs," pp. 369-370; Robert A. Aleshire, "Planning and Citizen Participation: Costs, Benefits, and Approaches," *Urban Affairs Quarterly* 5 (1970):369-393; and John Friedmann, *Retracking America: A Theory of Transactive Planning* (Garden City, N.Y.: Anchor, 1973).

49. Spiegel, "Citizen Participation in Federal Programs," pp. 369-370.

50. U.S. Senate, Committee on Governmental Affairs, *Public Participation in Regulatory Agency Proceedings,* 95th Congress, 1st Session, 1977, Prepared Pursuant to S. Res. 71.

51. Alinsky, *Rules for Radicals*; Verba and Nie, *Participation in America*; and Dale Rogers Marshall, "Who Participates in What? A Bibliographic Essay on Individual Participation in Urban Areas," *Urban Affairs Quarterly* 4 (1968):201-223.

52. Alinsky, *Rules for Radicals*; and Yin et al., *Citizen Organizations*.

53. Bell and Held, "The Community Revolution," and Perlman, "Grassrooting the System."

54. Robert Bailey, Jr., *Radicals in Urban Politics: The Alinsky Approach* (Chicago: University of Chicago Press, 1972).

55. Michael Lipsky, "Protest as a Political Resource," *American Political Science Review* 62 (1968):1144-1158.

56. Arnstein, "A Ladder of Citizen Participation"; Schmandt, "Decentralization"; Edmund M. Burke, "Citizen Participation Strategies," *Journal of the American Institute of Planners* 34 (1968):287-294; and Jon Van Til and Sally Bould Van Til, "Citizen Participation in Social Policy: The End of the Cycle?" *Social Problems* 17 (1970):313-323.

57. U.S. Department of Transportation, *Effective Citizen Participation*.

58. Advisory Commission on Intergovernmental Relations, *The New Grass Roots Government?*

59. Kasperson and Brietbart, *Participation*.

60. Lipset, *Political Man*; and Robert A. Dahl, *Who Governs? Democracy and Power in an American City* (New Haven: Yale University Press, 1961).

61. Bottomore, *Elites and Society*; and C. Wright Mills, *The Power Elite* (New York: Oxford University Press, 1956).

62. Sheldon S. Wolin, *Politics and Vision: Continuity and Innovation in Western Political Thought* (Boston: Little, Brown, 1960); Wilson C. McWilliams, *The Idea of Fraternity in America* (Berkeley: University of California Press, 1973); and Paul L. Levy, ed., *Justice and the City* (Philadelphia: Institute for the Study of Civic Values, 1977).

63. Stanley Elkins and Eric McKitrick, "A Meaning for Turner's Frontier," *Political Science Quarterly* 69 (1954):320-353 and 564-602; Merle Curti, *The Making of An American Community: A Case Study of Democracy in a Frontier County* (Palo Alto, Calif.: Stanford University Press, 1959); Frederick Jackson Turner, "The Significance of the Frontier in American History," in Frontier and Section: *Selected Essays of Frederick Jackson Turner* (Englewood Cliffs, N.J.: Prentice-Hall, 1961), pp. 37-62; and Robert R. Dykstra, *The Cattle Towns* (New York: Atheneum, 1970).

64. Paul Davidoff, "Advocacy and Pluralism in Planning," *Journal of the American Institute of Planners* 31 (1965):331-338.

65. Alan Lupo et al., *Rites of Way: The Politics of Transportation in Boston and the U.S. City* (Boston: Little, Brown, 1971); Julian Wolpert et al., *Metropolitan Neighborhoods: Participation and Conflict Over Change* (Washington: Association of American Geographers, 1972); Gordon Fellman with Barbara Brandt, *The Deceived Majority: Politics and Protest in Middle America* (New Brunswick: Transaction, 1973); and Chester Hartman, *Yerba Buena: Land Gram and Community Resistance in San Francisco* (San Francisco: Glide, 1975).

66. Lisa Peattie, "Reflections on Advocacy Planning," *Journal of the American Institute of Planners* 34 (1968):80-88.

67. Frances Fox Piven, "Whom Does the Advocate Planner Serve?" *Social Policy* 1 (1970):32-35, 37.

68. Friere, *Pedagogy of the Depressed*; Herbert Marcuse, *One Dimensional Man* (Boston: Beacon Press, 1964); and Ivan Illich, *Deschooling Society* (New York: Harper and Row, 1970).

69. Paul Davidoff, Linda Davidoff, and Neil Gold, "Suburban Action: Advocate Planning for an Open Society," *Journal of the American Institute of Planners* 36 (1970):12-21.

70. Spiegel, "Citizen Participation in Federal Programs"; and Martin L. Needleman and Carolyn Emerson Needleman, *Guerrillas in the Bureaucracy: The Community Planning Experiment in the United States* (New York: John Wiley, 1974).

4 Citizen Participation and Democratic Theory

Nelson M. Rosenbaum

Introduction

Over the past three decades, the process by which government decisions are made in the United States has profoundly changed. Starting with the Administrative Procedure Act of 1946, mandates and requirements for active citizen participation in administrative policy making have proliferated at all levels of government. In practice, these new requirements have been widely, if grudgingly, accepted by the administrators and bureaucrats to whom they are directed. While incompetence and inexperience have undercut the effectiveness of some citizen-participation exercises, outright bureaucratic obstreperousness has been held to a minimum.

Despite the practical acceptance, doubts about the theoretical legitimacy and appropriateness of citizen-participation requirements remain—not only among many bureaucrats, administrators, and legislators, but also among scholars and commentators on government. Some critics have challenged the spread of citizen participation as a "democratic distemper" at variance with the principles of democratic governance incorporated in the Constitution. Others have questioned the underlying assumption of citizen participation, that the "mass public" can define or defend its own interests in government decision making.

Is citizen participation justified by democratic principles? How does the expansion of participation rights fit in with traditional concepts of American government. How much participation is enough from the perspective of democratic theory? These and other issues of democratic theory are briefly addressed in this essay as an introduction to a most challenging and significant realm of political and philosophical debate.

Principles of Democratic Governance

There is little disagreement among theorists of democracy, both classical and contemporary, that two central values stand at the core of democratic practice: political equality and popular sovereignty. The argument between theorists lies not so much over what constitutes democratic principles, but rather over the degree to which the values of democracy are compatible with the stability, efficiency, and authority of the state. These "statist" values are not particularly associated with democracy, but rather are central concerns of any self-perpetuating state, be it the Third Reich or the United States.

Theoretical arguments over the clash of democratic and statist values are both normative and empirical in nature. Classical theorists generally argued on normative grounds, basing their arguments on assumptions about human nature and capacities. Contemporary theorists tend to argue on normative *and* empirical grounds, backing up conclusions about the legitimacy and feasibility of democracy with comparative and quantitative evidence on citizens' capacities and attitudes.

The first part of this essay will examine the normative groundwork of the two major democratic values in classical theory and the relationship of these values to the movement for expanded citizen participation in government. Succeeding sections will consider both normative and empirical critiques of citizen participation forwarded by contemporary theorists.

Equality

Political equality is the essential first principle of democratic governance. Political equality refers not to equal influence over government decisions, for this can be achieved only if the preferences of all citizens are known. Rather, the essential condition of democracy is that all citizens have an equal *opportunity* to exert infuence through political activity if they choose to do so. Through political equality, the full diversity of interests and values bearing on a problem can be brought into policy debate and can be incorporated into the final decision.

The essential corollary of the equality principle is rule of the majority. Among those who choose to participate, the preferences of no one citizen should be weighted more heavily than those of any other citizen. Decisions should be controlled by the greatest number expressing their preferences in favor of a particular alternative.[1]

Political equality is rationalized and justified by theorists of democracy on three major grounds. First, it is argued that interests and values are subjective and autonomous. Thus, it is essential that each citizen make his own choices. For example, G.D.H. Cole claims that no man can represent another accurately "because no man's will can be treated as a substitute for, or representative of, the wills of others."[2] Second, even if it is conceded that a citizen's interests and values can be represented without some act of direct political expression on his part, many theorists argue that individual political activity is the only way of insuring that these values are not disregarded. For example, John Stuart Mill notes: ". . . the rights and interests of every or any person are only secure from being disregarded when the person interested is himself able and habitually disposed to stand up for them.''[3] Finally, theorists of democracy justify political equality on the ground that it is only through individual political activity that individuals become fully aware of their responsibilities to society and gain the personal confidence that comes from shared control of public actions. Rousseau is perhaps the most prominent political theorist associated with this self-realization rationale for political equality.[4]

The extent to which this ideal conception of political equality is capable of implementation in American democratic practice has been at the core of political debate in the United States over its entire history. As contemporary "elite theorists" have so frequently noted, the initial resolution of this issue in the federal and state constitutions involved only a very limited acceptance of political equality.[5] Restrictions on the extent of the franchise reflected a distrust of the mass public and its potential destabilizing effect upon the authoritative functioning of the state.

Over the last two hundred years, a dramatic broadening of the cramped conception of political equality incorporated in the initial constitutions has taken place. Extension of the franchise to non-property owners, women, blacks, the young, and the poor has been successfully accomplished, but not without bitter struggle. Over the last several decades, the major battleground in the struggle for political equality has shifted toward the expansion of opportunities for citizen participation in administrative decision making. This struggle is animated by the same concerns and commitments that underlay the earlier battles over the franchise.

A major factor in the enactment of the original Administrative Procedure Act of 1946 and in most subsequent mandates for citizen involvement was the perception that the interests of most citizens were being disregarded by a group of decision-making institutions that increasingly affected important aspects of their lives. The pattern of co-optation and domination of administrative agencies by particular clientele groups that prevailed in the immediate postwar era has been thoroughly documented.[6] As the American public grew increasingly more affluent, educated, and organized in the 1950s and 1960s, this affront to political equality became increasingly intolerable. Thus, statutory mandates authorizing citizen participation have explicitly recognized the need to provide citizens with means of insuring administrative fairness and accountability through access to appeal procedures and the courts.

The theme of autonomy has also played a large role in the evolution of citizen-involvement requirements. Rejecting theories of public administration that claim that the "public interest" as a whole can somehow be defined by "neutral" and "disinterested" bureaucrats, legislators have recognized that it is only through the clash and conflict of the full diversity of affected interests that a reasonable approximation of responsive public policy can be developed. Thus, many citizen-participation mandates place special emphasis on reaching out to affected but inexperienced citizens who might otherwise not enjoy the opportunity to participate and whose specific interests might not be considered.

Finally, the desire to increase the sense of self-confidence and social responsibility on the part of alienated segments of American society has motivated at least some of the recent mandates for expanded participation in policy making. For example, citizen participation in the model cities and community action programs of the 1960s was based explicitly on the hypothesis that participation would counteract the sense of powerlessness among the poor and black segments of the population to which the programs were directed.[7]

In sum, the movement for expansion of citizen-participation rights and opportunities falls squarely within traditional concerns of democratic theory about equality of opportunity for political activity and influence. The movement may be viewed as the current manifestation of continuing evolution of American government and politics toward a closer approximation of the democratic ideal.

Sovereignty

The principle of popular sovereignty denotes that government is a creation *of* the citizenry rather than a separate entity standing above it. Democratic government is self-government—that is, government that derives from and responds to the wishes of the people. Government must do no more and no less than the people desire.

This vision of democratic practice is defended by political theorists on two major grounds. First, it is argued by Rousseau, Mill, and others that political obligation can only legitimately derive from an individual's feeling of voluntary association with the state and his satisfaction that government is ultimately responsive to his needs and interests. This does not mean that every interest can be satisfied all the time. Even Rousseau concedes that the general will must at times override the particular will under conditions of conflict. However, over the long term, the state must be sufficiently sensitive and responsive to the needs of its people so that all share a sense of mutual commitment. Second, many theorists argue that the most effective defense of liberty is achieved through the principle of popular sovereignty. If it is in the self-interest of citizens to maximize their own freedom, then how can citizens tyrannize themselves? While democratic theorists generally agree that limitations and constraints on the power of the state must be guaranteed through constitutions and laws, they maintain that the ultimate source of limited government is the people themselves.[8] The laws of a democratic state are only as effective as the values and interests of its citizens.

As in the realm of political equality, American democracy did not begin with a great deal of respect for the principle of popular sovereignty. While the initial federal and state constitutions were based officially upon the concept of popular sovereignty, provision for popular sovereignty in practice was quite limited. Many of the founders distrusted the passions of ordinary men and strove to insulate government from popular pressure and direction. Madison, for example, was skeptical of majority tyranny and sought to constrain government by laws and by checks and balances rather than by the values and commitments of men. Elaborate processes of representation, such as indirect election of senators, were written into the constitutions to further dilute the principle of popular sovereignty. Heavy reliance was placed upon an independent appointed judiciary to serve as the guardian of liberty and the arbiter of obligation.

This initial conception of popular sovereignty has changed dramatically over the course of American political history, particularly over the last eighty years. During the nineteenth century, the number of public officials subject to popular election increased dramatically, culminating symbolically in direct election of U.S. senators. In the early twentieth century, the mechanisms of direct popular intervention in legislative decision making (initiative, referendum) were developed and widely disseminated. The mechanism of recall was also introduced as a means for citizens to prevent and eliminate abuses of authority on the part of elected officials.

In the postwar era, following directly from the earlier victories, the main thrust of efforts to implement popular sovereignty has been the development of requirements for citizen participation in administrative decision making. The enormous growth in the power and discretion of administrative agencies during the postwar era constitutes one of the most profound challenges to the principle of popular sovereignty confronted in the political history of the United States. While formally accountable to the legislature and elected executives, modern bureaucracies have become so massive and pervasive that they have largely escaped careful and continuous oversight by these representative institutions. The courts have been active over the past thirty years in assessing whether administrative agencies have acted arbitrarily or capriciously, but, of course, they can only adjudicate cases and controversies that are brought to them. In many respects, then, the authorization of citizen participation represents a cry for help on the part of legislators and executives—that is, a recognition that representative institutions and courts cannot do the entire job of insuring the responsiveness of administrative agencies without the direct assistance and involvement of ordinary citizens.

The need for increasing the citizen's sense of political obigation also underlies many recent mandates for citizen participation. Citizen resistance to what is perceived as arbitrary decision making by distant bureaucracies is a serious problem in many areas of public administration. It is assumed by legislators and administrators that greater participation in the formulation of decisions will lead to greater citizen satisfaction and greater willingness to support administrative policies.[9] Thus, the basic theme of popular sovereignty and political obligation that runs throughout the history of democratic thought has been rediscovered and implemented in contemporary administrative practice.

Limits to Democracy

As with previous surges of democratic values during the Jacksonian and Progressive eras, the current expansion of participation rights and opportunities in the realm of administrative decision making has unleashed concern about efficiency, stability, and authority and has been subjected to vigorous criticism about "excesses" of democracy. In this section, the major empirical critiques of citizen participation and the alternative normative theories presented by critics are discussed.

The Critique of Participation

One of the facets of citizen participation in decision making that troubles critics most is its alleged inefficiency in identifying public preferences and aggregating them into coherent public policy. Citizen participation can be extremely costly, unwieldy, and time-consuming. Enormous amounts of information must be distributed and explained, everyone must have an adequate chance to express his preferences, appeals must be heard, and so forth. Ordinary citizens often do not understand complex issues the first time around and must be patiently led through the maze on multiple occasions. Critics also claim that many ordinary citizens have no definite preferences (and should not be expected to have any) regarding policy issues that may affect them in some way but are not immediately salient.[10] Unsuccessful attempts to "reach out" to uninvolved and apathetic citizens during the community action and model cities programs are often cited as evidence of the inability of ordinary citizens to participate meaningfully in defining and defending their own interests.

Perhaps even more serious than the waste of time and money in attempting to stimulate the expression of preferences among those who have none is the inefficiency inherent in attempting to aggregate the outpouring of views and opinions with which administrators are confronted.

How should preferences be weighed? Does a casual answer on a survey questionnaire count the same as a thoughtful presentation at a public meeting? How can general expressions of preference be related to specific policy proposals? Unfortunately, there rarely are clear answers to these questions, nor explicit decision rules to guide administrators in coping with citizen opinions. Lacking clear rules and methods for resolving conflicting preferences, administrators often make decisions that are challenged and appealed, thus causing more delay and expense.

A second common criticism of citizen participation is that rather than increasing the sense of political obligation and support for government, as proponents suggest, participation often results in ever greater instability and discontent. Many critics focus upon the danger of overloading the political system with irresponsible demands for services and subsidies that government cannot realistically provide. The inflation of expectations precipitated by citizen participation creates increased dissatisfaction and unrest when demands are not met.[11] Other commentators question the hypothesis that greater participation necessarily leads to greater satisfaction with the political system. A few preliminary studies indicate that participation *per se* demonstrates little association with trust and support.[12] Rather, it is substantive satisfaction with a decision that leads to faith in the political system.

Finally, a number of critics charge that citizen-participation mandates have undermined governmental authority to the point that institutions are no longer able to act decisively and effectively. The widespread grant of standing to obtain judicial review has provided an effective veto power over administrative actions to small groups that do not reflect the will of the majority. Citizen-participation requirements have demoralized creative bureaucrats and administrators and have prevented them from utilizing their expertise and experience in solving problems. Decisions tend to reflect the lowest common denominator—the minimum acceptable alternative to all groups and individuals—rather than the best judgment of knowledgeable officials. Perhaps most significantly, citizen participation has eroded the power of representative institutions, which are now frequently bypassed as administrators engage in direct contact and negotiation with members of the public.

Alternative Theories

As an alternative to the surge of democratic values involved in the expansion of citizen-participation opportunities, critics generally offer a formula for "mixed government" that places greater emphasis upon the maintenance of efficiency, stability, and authority. In essence, the alternative formulations reflect the so-called elite theory of democracy postulated by theorists like Michels, Schumpeter, and Lippman earlier in this century.[13] While most descriptions of elite theory are vastly oversimplified, the essence of this approach is that the role of ordinary citizens in a democracy is appropriately limited to periodic election of leaders who can represent and defend citizens' interests more effectively than they can themselves. In Schumpeter's celebrated definition, democracy is "that institutional arrangement for arriving at political decisions in which individuals acquire the power to decide by means of a competitive struggle for the people's vote."[14] Through the leadership of elected officials, the interests and values of citizens can be effectively represented with far greater efficiency and far less danger to stability and authority than under conditions of direct democracy.

In line with these principles, contemporary critics of citizen participation typically stress a revitalization of representative institutions as the primary means of coping with the challenge to responsiveness and accountability presented by the growth of administrative power. Critics agree that the citizen role should be primarily indirect—mediated through elections, interest groups, and political parties. The focus of democratic practice is on transmitting information about interests and needs through these mechanisms to the elected officials who can responsibly act upon them. The critics of participation disagree, however, on the most appropriate institution for the exercise of administrative guidance and oversight.

Most theorists focus upon a resurgence of legislative authority, expressed through decreased delegation of discretion in statutory enactments, closer oversight of administrative operations, and greater intervention in specific instances of rulemaking.[15] A number of theorists express great admiration for the flexibilty of legislatures—their capacity for trade-off and compromise of interests. Others are attracted by the authoritative character of legislative action as a means of enforcing responsiveness to public needs and interests—as contrasted to the problematic impact of citizen participation upon administrative decision making.

Some critics, on the other hand, emphasize the need for revitalization of executive leadership and control over the bureaucracy.[16] The executive, in this view, is better able to get involved in the day-to-day details of public administration and can direct the bureaucracy in a more coherent manner than can fragmented legislative committees. Emphasis on the executive role in asserting popular control of administration is frequently accompanied by paeans to political parties as the most appropriate means for ascertaining and aggregating the interests of the public and holding the executive accountable for his guidance of the bureaucracy.

Conclusions

Unlike earlier episodes of political and philosophical debate over the democratization of our governmental institutions, the controversy over citizen participation in administrative decision making does not really present a hard choice between incompatible alternatives. In many respects, an increase in citizen participation and a revitalization of representative institutions are complementary as means of insuring responsiveness and accountability on the part of administrative agencies. It is the respective emphasis that should be placed on each approach that forms the essential core of the theoretical and empirical dispute.

Proponents of citizen participation build upon the continuous evolution of the American political system toward a greater respect for democratic values. In effect, there is a systematic bias toward democratization enforced both by historic tradition and belief in the inevitability and desirability of change and reform. As critics have legitimately noted, however, the theoretical rationale of citizen participation may be based on artificial and idealized expectations about the common man and may not fully anticipate the implications of participation for the functioning of the state. In some cases, there have been "excesses" of democracy which have required corrective action. For example, the approach to citizen participation in the model cities program was terminated by Congress when it appeared that an enormous expenditure of time and money produced little in the way of constructive, representative input from disadvantaged citizens. Similarly, Congress terminated further judicial appeals of the Alaska pipeline case when it appeared that small advocacy groups were using access to the courts to frustrate the implementation of a decision that enjoyed widespread popular support.

On the other hand, critics of citizen participation unquestionably overstate their case and overgeneralize from a few prominent instances of excess. The impact of citizen involvement upon the citizen's sense of political obligation has not yet been fully and fairly tested under a variety of conditions and circumstances. While it is easy to condemn the delays and the undermining of authority involved in judicial appeals of administrative action, critics also fail to acknowledge the high proportion of cases in which citizen complaints of arbitrary, inconsistent, or illegal action have been validated by the courts. Citizens may, indeed, become the most effective defenders of their own liberty, as Mill claimed, if they are provided the proper tools. In addition, most critics fail to acknowledge at all one of the most important functions of citizen participation—the development of a sense of self-confidence and responsibility. Although available evidence is not conclusive, enough research has been completed to indicate that the self-realization effect of participation in decision making is strong and consistent.[17]

While the critics of citizen participation present a posture of hardheaded realism in their attacks on idealized democratic values, the idea that representative institutions can carry the full load of insuring responsiveness and accountability may be even more unrealistic. In theory, an increase in the vigor of representative institutions is highly desirable. To the extent that legislators and executives can define priorities with some precision, oversee legislative agencies to insure that they are responsive to citizen needs, and intervene with their full weight in cases of arbitrary and unresponsive decision making, the strengthening of legislative institutions is complementary with citizen participation rather than in conflict. Citizens as individuals or organized in groups cannot fulfill these broad functions effectively. At best, they can clumsily use the courts to push administrative agencies in a particular direction. However, it is highly unrealistic to expect representative institutions to enjoy the detailed knowledge or the time and interest to get involved in the day-to-day bureaucratic struggles that constitute the core of citizen participation. Indeed, as previously noted, many citizen-involvement mandates represent an explicit acknowledgment by legislators and executives that citizens know their own specific interests best and are best suited to defend them in administrative combat.

In sum, as in any period of extensive change in our democratic institutions, we face a set of fundamental questions about the theoretical justification and legitimacy of reform. This essay has attempted to show that the movement for expanded citizen participation in government falls in the mainstream of democratic throught and American traditions. Some rethinking of initial efforts to democratize administrative agencies is necessary to insure that an adequate level of government efficiency, stability, and authority is maintained. However, the basic thrust of democratization underlying citizen participation is unlikely to be deflected. To the extent that suggestions for strengthening the role of representative institutions in administrative decision making can be implemented, this approach will complement and reinforce rather than supplant the movement for citizen participation.

Notes

1. On the derivation of the decision rules from the classical postulate of political equality, see Robert Dahl, *A Preface to Democratic Theory* (Chicago: University of Chicago Press, 1956), pp. 63-90.

2. G.D.H. Cole, *Social Theory* (London, England: Methune, 1920), p. 103, quoted in Hanna Pitkin, *The Concept of Representation* (Berkeley: University of California Press, 1960), p. 207.

3. John Stuart Mill, *Consideration of Representative Government* (Chicago: Henry Regnery Edition, 1962), p. 58.

4. J.J. Rousseau, *The Social Contract* (Chicago: Henry Regnery Edition, 1954), Book II. An incisive treatment of Rousseau's "Of Self-Realization" is found in Carol Pateman, *Participation and Democratic Theory* (Cambridge, England: Cambridge University Press, 1970), pp. 22-44. See also Mill, *Consideration of Representative Government,* pp. 60-74.

5. See Martin Diamond, *Consideration of Representative Government,* "The Declaration and the Constitution: Liberty, Democracy, and the Founders," *The Public Interest* 41 (1975):39-55.

6. See Marver Bernstein, *Regulatory Business by Independent Commission* (Princeton: Princeton University Press, 1955); Grant McConnell, *Private Power and American Democracy* (New York: Random House, 1966).

7. On the origins of the effort to counteract alienation through the community action program, see Paul Peterson, "Forms of Representation: Participation of the Poor in the Community Action Program," *American Political Science Review* 64 (1970):491-508.

8. Mill, *Consideration of Representative Government,* Chapter 3. This view, of course, was explicitly rejected by the framers of the Constitution, who distrusted the potential for majority tyranny as well as the propensity of ordinary men to be swayed by despots and demagogues. See *The Federalist Papers,* Nos. 10 and 37.

9. The derivation of this hypothesis in modern small group theory, as well as in classical political thought, is discussed in Sidney Verba, *Small Groups in Political Behavior* (Princeton: Princeton University Press, 1960). See also Pateman, *Participation and Democratic Theory,* pp. 45-85. On the importance of this hypothesis in generating mandates for citizen involvement, see Daniel Mazmanian, "Participatory Democracy in a Federal Agency," in John Pierce and Harvey Doerksen, eds., *Water Politics and Public Involvement* (Ann Arbor, Mich.: Science Publishers, 1976).

10. See Robert Dahl, "Further Reflections on 'The Elitist Theory of Democracy'," *American Political Science Review* 60 (1966):296-305; Robert Nisbet, "Public Opinion vs. Popular Opinion," *The Public Interest* 41 (1975):166-192.

11. Samuel P. Huntington, "The Democratic Distemper," *The Public Interest* 41 (1975):9-38; Daniel P. Moynihan, *Maximum Feasible Misunderstanding* (New York: The Free Press, 1970).

12. Mazmanian, "Participatory Democracy"; Richard Cole, *Citizen Participation and the Urban Political Process* (Lexington, Mass.: Lexington Books, D.C. Heath and Company, 1974); Nelson Rosenbaum, *Citizens and Land Use Policy* (Washington: The Urban Institute, forthcoming.)

13. There is, of course, no single "elite theory" of democracy. The term is used, however, to describe a number of theorists who hold roughly similar views on the limits of popular participation in decision making. See Jack Walker, "A Critique of the Elitist Theory of Democracy," *American Political Science Review* 60 (1966):285-295, and Dennis Thompson, *The Democratic Citizen* (Cambridge, England: Cambridge University Press, 1970), for a description and analysis of elite theorists.

14. Joseph Schumpeter, *Capitalism, Socialism and Democracy* (New York: Harper and Brothers, 1942), p. 296.

15. One of the most influential general statements of this approach is found in Theodore Lowy, *The End of Liberalism* (New York: Norton, 1969). A strong argument for revitalization of legislative institutions, vis a vis citizen participation in the specific area of sensitive policy is made in Edwin Haefele, *Representative Government for Environmental Management* (Baltimore, Maryland: Johns Hopkins University Press for R.F.F., 1973).

16. Huntington, "The Democratic Distemper"; Moynihan, *Maximum Feasible Misunderstanding*; D. Stephen Cupps, "Energy Problems of Citizen Participation," *Public Administration Review* 38 (1978).

17. Dale Rogers Marshall, *The Politics of Participation and Poverty* (Berkeley: University of California Press, 1971); Cole, *Social Theory*; Pateman, *Participation and Democratic Theory.*

5 The Public-Interest Movement and Citizen Participation

David Cohen

Incongruity is a feature of American society. The nonfiction best-seller lists are full of books about self-improvement, while voluntary service groups continue to thrive.[1] Fewer voters identify themselves with political parties now, although ongoing attempts are being made to strengthen our national and congressional parties. Special interests proliferate, organize their fund-raising campaign committees,[2] and pursue their demands, yet a national public-interest constituency matures.[3] The percentage of eligible voters who go to the polls goes downhill steadily,[4] as interest and involvement in issue politics sharpen in intensity. Paralysis prevents problem solving at the same time that leaders with a problem-solving style draw voter support. Public confidence in government plummets at the same time that citizens win important battles to improve government accountability. It is in the context of these contrast that the public-interest constituency has injected a new dimension into American politics, particularly by placing issues on the national, state, and local agendas. Will this important new constituency be able to continue this role?

The Vietnam War and Watergate were as important to the development of the public-interest constituencies as the depression was for the Roosevelt constituency. Vietnam and Watergate have brought to the surface basic questions about our past assumptions of high trust in public officials. The facile optimism of earlier days has vanished. Instead, a skepticism about finding workable solutions to difficult problems has permeated the political scene. The steadily eroding effects of inflation increase the temptation for people to turn inward and away from communitarian approaches to our public concerns. The challenge for the public-interest movement is to overcome the paralysis and malaise that dominate the public arena.

In the 1970s, public-interest groups have had an important impact on our political institutions. These groups are a force apart from the political parties and are outside the tradtional economic groupings. They have provided leadership in helping to place issues on the national political agenda. They have battled the older and more traditional interest groups and at times have bested them. Even more important, they have helped to stretch the outer limits of what is politically possible. In so doing, they have become an essential part of the resurgence of citizen participation in the 1970s.

The public-interest groups have had an impact on issues that reflect im-

55

portant changes in American politics. The Roosevelt coalition is burned
out, and with it the liberalism that spanned the period from the New Deal to
the Great Society. At present, the new majority is far from established, yet
when it coalesces, it is bound to include some of the emerging public-
interest constituencies.

The rise and establishment of the public-interest movement is closely
linked to issue politics—the practice of people organizing themselves
around issues and lobbying for them. Although the concept of issue politics
is rooted in American political history, in the past it was seldom separate
from candidate politics or political parties. Both the civil-rights and the
ban-the-bomb movements were early examples of the newer form of issue
politics that has developed since World War II. But issue politics is not
limited to those who are trying to bring about change; it is also practiced by
those who resist social change. The anti-ERA movement, the right-to-life
movement, and, in earlier years, the angry reactions to the decisions of the
U.S. Supreme Court under Chief Justice Earl Warren, in which defenders
of the status quo called for nullification of desegregation and "one-person-
one-vote" decisions, are also examples of issue politics.

The Difference between Issue Politics and the Public-Interest Movement

Although they are closely linked, issue politics and the public-interest movement must be distinguished from each other. Issue politics is the practice of
organizing around issues, no matter what values are involved. The public-
interest movement—consumer, environmentalist, government reform,
institution-related professionals—deals with those questions that are not
ethnically, racially, sectionally, economically, or occupationally dominant.
To sustain its influence, the public-interest constituency must not claim to
practice a politics of superiority, a politics of morality, or a politics of vir-
tue. The public-interest movement is basically an attempt at restoring
representational balance in our public institutions. It strives to change our
system by building a place for those voices that are often unheard. It deals
with the question of who is represented and who is excluded in our political
system—who gets attention and who is ignored. It is as presumptuous and
arrogant to believe that any specific group or individual has a monopoly on
representing the public interest as it is to assert that any one remedy clearly
represents the public interest.

Public-interest groups must stay in touch with their grassroots sup-
porters. If that important link is not maintained, their accountability to a
constituency vanishes, and their public credibility is quickly lost.

Public-interest organizations are often defined as groups that seek
"common, collective, or public goods" that do not exclusively, materially,

or selectively benefit their members. Open government, clean air, and freedom of information are examples of collective goods. Similarly, if a public-interest group deals with policies that affect wages, entitlement, or an ability to compete in the marketplace, a broad spectrum of citizens is likely to benefit from its effects. The results will neither selectively nor exclusively reward its own members.

The diffused benefits of public-interest activities need to be contrasted to the benefits accruing to the special interests as a result of their activities. Specialized interests, such as health, energy, or construction groups, claim that their good is also the public's good. After all, they provide the goods and services for society and regular paychecks for workers. There are, however, significant limits to this claim.

The central objective of these special interests and their activities is certainly their own success. When a contest between their immediate concerns and the interest of the community arises, the community is left to fend for itself. This basic fact of life is why the public-interest movement is necessary. The simple fact that a chemical company pays its workers does not mean that these workers must accept sterilization. Simply because a mill produces steel, must those living nearby accept emphysema? The production of goods and services does not mean that business should be anticompetitive or should be allowed to influence govermental decision unduly. The activities of a public-interest constituency exist to advocate the larger public objectives left unrepresented by these narrow interests.

The objective of seeking accountability in government decision making is to ensure that unheard voices have a chance to be listened to while organizations are enabled to pursue matters that do substantially benefit their constituents alone. By widening access to public institutions and shifting power relationships among those who influence decision makers, accountability affects decisions that will be ultimately made.

Creating government accountability requires building competition into our political system, enabling citizens to know what's happening, correcting political abuses of power, guarding against lapses of integrity, and fostering institutional competence. All these are central to a democracy. In short, an open and fluid process is necessary to ensure that citizens will be listened to on a sustained basis.

Some Historic Roots of the Public-Interest Movement

The public-interest movement emerged in the 1960s after Congress had enacted a spate of legislation to take care of unfinished business going back to the New Deal days. Its leading participants are those who concentrate on governmental-reform, environmental, and consumer issues. These movements all began building citizen support within the same few years. Their near-simultaneous emergence led to the recognition of public-interest groups as a political force. Although the public-interest community represents a variety of interests, with approaches and political styles that sometimes conflict, these three basic components are strongly linked.

It is worth examining the institutional and political reasons for the emergence of these three movements. From the 1930s to the 1960s, the Roosevelt coalition—working-class people, city residents, blacks, southerners, and university-associated people—dominated presidential politics. The rural areas, thinly populated and economically underdeveloped, dominated Congress. In the House of Representatives, most states were malapportioned. The Senate was dominated by the South and by sparsely populated western states. (At the end of World War II, 15 of 33 Senate committee chairmen were from the South.) As a result, the presidency was the center of action that generated proposals, while the Congress all too often played the negative role of blocking these proposals by inaction.

An institutional paralysis had afflicted Congress and was preventing the government from dealing effectively with national problems. The House Rules Committee refused to permit major issues to be voted on by the full House of Representatives. The Senate's filibuster rule allowed a minority of the Senate to prevent the majority from deciding issues. The result was a legislative veto of such major policy initiatives as civil-rights legislation, federal aid to education, and Medicare. A congressional minority was able to put such crucial issues on the back burner. Dedicated to preserving the status quo, it postponed dealing with national problems and correcting glaring inequities.

This stalemate lasted for more than 25 years—from after the 1938 congressional elections to the presidency of Lyndon Johnson. The sudden outpouring of legislation under Johnson flooded the administrative channels of the executive branch. The government was just not equipped to deliver the services promised by the myriad of new laws that were enacted in such areas as housing, education, health, and jobs.

During the years of the mid-1960s, the political situation was volatile and confusing. Efforts were being made to deal all at once with a host of important issues—poverty, discrimination, racism, cities, war, and taxes. Each new law created a new set of rights. Expectations were high, but performance in administering and enforcing these new laws too often was low. When the inner-city residents of Watts, Detroit, and Newark let their resentment explode in riots, the unexpected shock shifted the mood of the nation from a politics of hope to a politics of despair. The national spirit was further depressed by the oppressive pall of the Vietnam War, which hung over everything. Distrust and cynicism about American ideals were omnipresent.

Confidence in institutions tumbled, as the percentage who voted of those eligible declined in each successive presidential election after 1960 and in congressional elections after 1962. As increasing numbers of voters abandoned party preference, it appeared that many citizens were simply withdrawing from politics. In fact, the initial protests against the Vietnam War had all the appearance of avoiding, rather than engaging in, politics.

By the late 1960s, the Roosevelt political coalition was hopelessly fractured. Its members were intensely divided on questions of war and peace. On its domestic agenda there were equally severe tensions involving questions of race and the distribution of economic and social benefits. Few issues remained on which the component parts of the old coalition were still united. Exaggerated promises, coupled with a lack of visible progress, compounded the tensions. The only tangible results of the mid-1960s legislative boom appeared to be the benefits in public accommodations and voting rights brought about by the Civil Rights Act.

The fracturing of the Roosevelt coalition—its last hurrah was the 1968 Hubert Humphrey presidential campaign—led to the start of a new mix in our political system. Organized constituencies began to form in support of long-neglected issues. The consumer and environmental movements are the most obvious examples. They became involved in both issue and candidate politics, but at arm's length from the established political parties. At the same time, new players and leaders emerged from the Office of Economic Opportunity programs, as Head Start mothers and others who had learned they had a right to a say on delivery of services began to speak up. As all these groups demanded to be heard, they created a new pressure to build accountability into our public and private institutions. Within the medical and legal professions, which had long concentrated chiefly on their own professional and economic interests, a new constituency began to develop that looked beyond those immediate concerns to the social responsibilities of their respective professions.

The defenders of traditional interests were thrown off stride by the new consumer and environmental efforts. By the old standards, the new groups seemed to operate apart from politics. Nothing could be more misleading. It was issue politics, not candidate politics, that they practiced, and they pursued that kind of politics far beyond election day.

As the movement grew, its participants discovered that the tired old political system had ossified. It couldn't bend. Government had become an insider's game. As government programs and machinery grew in complexity, the regulated industries and their regulators were able to manipulate the results, while citizens with consumer, environmental, and minority concerns were left largely on the outside. Governmental institutions, particularly the Congress, were incapable of handling or were unwilling to deal with the major issues, as politicians ducked the controversial questions, such as the

Vietnam War. Both the Senate and the House of Representatives as institutions refused to take a stand. In fact, the House's procedures were so hopelessly paralyzed and unresponsive that it was incapable of voting on the war issue until 1971.

This setting of institutional paralysis, combined with the shock of helplessness about Vietnam and the disappointment of high social and racial hopes as the vaunted programs worked poorly or not at all, triggered efforts at institutional overhaul and improved governmental accountability. The irony is that as the percentage of voting participation declined, there was an increase in citizen action at all levels. The workability of a large part of our system was being tested by the many citizen participants.

The Role of Public-Interest Groups in a Society

In the broadest sense, the public-interest movement involves the citizen's right to know, their ability to influence choices before they are narrowed to only one or two, and their influence in remedying abuses of power. It requires rising above short-run interests and looking at long-term consequences. The public-interest constituency has developed sophistication about the power and influence of special interest. Its members, in pursing their own special interests and community activities, are thwarted by institutional paralysis. But rather than accept the paralysis or incompetence or fumbling about, they seek to correct it by making demands for a better political system.

The public-interest constituency has political influence. It has played a key role in unmasking procedures, in developing new approaches to institutional representation, and in building new modes of political participation. The influence of the public-interest contituency will continue to last if it can push issues onto political agendas so that they are faced by our public representatives rather than shunted aside.

To succeed, a public-interest group must operate as a modern organization dealing with issues that matter to people, consulting with its members, focusing its constituencies and energies, respecting the professional role of the media by providing them with accurate and useful information, and paying attention to administrative management. (Failure to pay attention to administrative management will snuff out all good intentions. The public interest constituency will need its share of MBA's, just as it needed creative lawyers, imaginative researchers, skilled lobbyists, and inventive activists.)

There are a number of arenas of action for the public-interest constituency that apply whether national, state, or local issues are being dealt with.

Campaigns are one important arena for action, although campaign results alone neither block issues nor guarantee their passage. The ideal use of a campaign is to enlarge the political dialogue and to seek commitments from candidates, in the hope that these commitments will become promises that the winners feel bound to keep.

The other prime arenas of action are legislative bodies, executive bodies, independent agencies, and the courts. Regarding the operations of each of these institutions, a number of basic questions go to the heart of democratic practice:

1. Are their proceedings open to the public?
2. Are they accessible and responsive to different parts of the community?
3. Within each, is power diffused so that official judgments are products of deliberation?
4. Can they reach decisions without being sidetracked when a majority of members is ready to act?
5. Are positions of service in these institutions available on a competitive basis to all parts of society, or are they exclusive clubs for the favored?
6. Are their decisions communicated to and understood by the various publics they serve?

These questions are basic tests of accountability. Only when the institutions can answer yes to all these questions will leaders be able to lead and will the various publics be taken seriously.

Basic Elements for a Healthy Public-Interest Movement

The public-interest constituencies can't kid themselves. In unmasking procedures, developing new approaches to institutional representation, and building new modes of political participation, they are altering power and power relationships. They must be prepared for unanticipated consequences and they must remember that the latest reform adopted is often tomorrow's abuse. Care and professionalism are as essential for the public-interest advocates as for their special-interest adversaries.

The lessons of recent years suggest that a healthy political system requires an open decision-making process and well-organized, effective citizen action as a bulwark against a government that is dominated and influenced by a variety of special interests that have mastered the rules and procedures and often have exclusive access to certain public officials. Public-interest organizations must possess skills to promote and sustain open government as well as being able to compete honorably and effectively for the public interest.

Public-interest groups use a variety of mixes and blends of citizen action. They combine action with information, and couple activities inside the halls of Congress and elsewhere in government with pressures from outside these arenas. This involves fighting specific battles, which have beginnings and endings. It requires allies at all levels, including inside government, who will support an issue even if it is not a top priority for all allies. It requires debate and discussion, and it welcomes conflict as necessary in a democracy. It works at building majorities rather than tilting at ideological windmills. It shapes and sets an agenda rather than accepting the status quo. It teaches skills without dampening enthusiasm and freshness of approach. And it combines the enthusiasm of volunteers with the skill of professionals.

Professionalism must be a key style of operation for the public-interest constituency. Professionalism is important in formulating issues and remedies, including the use of original investigatory work and litigative targets. Hard-data reports, demonstrating the need for action on an issue, and the use of litigation are tools that will in turn lead to citizen-action lobbying.

The public-interest movement must accept the demanding role of agenda setter and watchdog. It is involved in issue politics, not above it. It has to give and take and not be rigid. Otherwise, it is plainly not a participant. Agenda setting means seeing that decision makers deal with issues that they would prefer to avoid for reasons ranging from political convenience to a deliberate escape from responsibility. Watchdogging is the necessary way of letting decision makers know that citizens intend to be involved in implementation as well as in setting of policies.

In issue politics, patience is essential. Issues take a long time to germinate. Citizens must combine professionalism in issue management with persistence and stamina. These are the necessary antidotes to the kind of mischievous utopianism and messianism that sometimes overtakes reform movements.

The Future of the Public-Interest Movement

The challenge for public-interest groups is to build on a politics of hope rather than on a politics of denunciation. It is unwise for the public-interest constituency to speculate about or to seek to create an alternative political party. The strength of the public-interest constituency depends on not maneuvering for its own electoral power. Its credibility results from battling for issues and for change without any hidden agendas.

In this setting, citizens have the ability to overcome the experts' domination of vital issues. Conflict, debate, and discussion lead to understanding and recognition of the various shared interests. But to succeed, such a process requires openness and public participation so that healthy institutions are built. Citizens must be able to know what's going on. Only then will our public officials be able to lead, govern, and decide critical questions. They will be in a position to emphasize the building of agreement out of shared interests in the larger community rather than fragmenting them as too often happens now.

Accountability is neither the politics of gesture nor the politics of quick accommodation, but rather involves painstaking attempts to provide access points to citizens so that institutional arrangements and power relationships are profoundly altered. Under a process that is accountable to the public, important choices will not be abandoned to the experts. Establishing modes of public participation will permit the nongovernmental sector to take an active part in the formulation of public goals. None of these steps is easy. American society will surely continue to change rapidly, and policies that are appropriate to one period in time will soon be overtaken by events. This is to be expected. Staleness comes, however, when the policies acquire a life of their own and will not be budged. Because the structure of our pluralistic, democratic form of government strongly favors special-interest policies over holistic policies, the public-interest constituency has a vital role to play. As an agenda setter and watchdog, it must continue to press government to take a comprehensive approach to policy setting while working toward active and appropriate participation by citizens.

It is important to recognize both the limitations of the public-interest constituency and where its best opportunities lie. Our most urgent challenge is to seek to build a society motivated by a sense of public purpose; a society based on hope, vision, and confidence; one that respects its institutions and is proud of them; a society that shares values and has a sense of the greater good.

Notes

1. The 1974 U.S. Census survey showed that 34 million people volunteered that year, with an average work week of nine hours.

2. Number of political action committees (PACs) and their growth rate (*Congressional Quarterly,* April 8, 1978, p. 853):

Date	Total	Corporate	Labor	Other
Dec. 31, 1974	608	89	201	318
Nov. 24, 1975	722	139	226	357
Dec. 31, 1976	1146	433	224	489
Dec. 31, 1977	1298	538	216	544

3. According to a 1976 study by Andrew Bavas, of the University of Illinois, there were 774 watchdog groups, including local chapters of national organizations, in the United States. Forty-four percent of these groups have been established since 1961, and 20 percent since 1971. Andrew Bavas, "Summary Report: A National Survey of Citizens' Watchdog Operations" (Chicago: Center for Urban Studies, University of Illiois at Chicago Circle, 1976).

4. Voter participation in presidential elections:

Year	Total	% Voter Turnout
1960	69 million	64
1964	71 million	61
1968	73 million	60
1972*	78 million	55
1976	82 million	54

*In 1972, the age limit for voting in presidential elections was lowered from 21 to 18.

Obviously, the percentage of turnout is the key data. Since 1962, similar declining percentages in off-year elections can be found.

6 Grassroots Participation from Neighborhood to Nation

Janice E. Perlman

The past decade has witnessed an unprecedented increase in the number, scope, and type of grassroots groups in this country. Building on a neighborhood base reaching all the way to multistate coalitions, and dealing with national issues, these groups are striving to make existing institutions more accountable and to gain increased control over the decisions that affect their lives.

Throughout the country, people are forming and joining grassroots groups, not simply as *ad hoc* defenses against external threats, but as an ongoing effort toward formulating and promoting their own positive agendas and programs. These actions represent bottom-up efforts of people taking collective actions on their own behalf, and they involve the use of a sophisticated blend of confrontation and cooperation in order to achieve their ends. Having arisen precisely because of the failures of both representative democracy and governmentally mandated citizen participation to reflect the needs of low- and moderate-income people, these grassroots groups are an emerging social force with the dynamism and potential to provide a most effective and meaningful form of citizen participation.

The Grassroots Movement in the 1970s

The contemporary grassroots movement is new, growing, diverse, and effective. Although its lineage can be traced back to the social movements of the 1960s, the early Alinsky organizations of the 1950s, and the union struggles of the 1930s and 1940s, in its present form it is not yet a decade old. Most of the groups we shall be describing started in the early 1970s, and many are five years old or less. They are growing in numbers and expanding in size so rapidly that any estimates of their size and numbers are outdated as quickly as they are calculated.

Equally dramatic has been their expansion in scope and their ability to organize simultaneously on multiple levels—from tenants' unions, to block clubs, to neighborhood associations, to city-wide and state-wide coalitions, to multistate and regional alliances, to a national movement. They follow the range of the issues that affect them and move adeptly back and forth from problems on the block to those of federal policy.

65

To achieve this flexibility, the grassroots groups effectively employ an array of elements, which are combined to meet their specific needs. They draw on traditional neighborhood association models, using local "turf" loyalties; on the direct-action tactics of social protest; on the boycott models of the farmworkers; on the expose methods of the public-interest lobbies; on service-delivery and economic-development skills; on local self-reliance and appropriate technologies; and on the new needs for program design, implementation, and monitoring that have emerged with the decentralization of federal and local government initiatives. In order to do this, they tread an extremely delicate line between conflict and consensus, between protest and partnership, and between principle and pragmatism. Whereas the issue of the 1960s was social justice and the rhetoric was revolutionary, the issue of the 1970s is economic justice and the rhetoric is reformist. The issues are more rooted in the specific facts of people's daily lives. The support base for such groups includes low- and moderate-income people across racial lines who join on issues of common interest and who are more interested in "making life" than "making history."

Citizen Action versus Citizen Involvement

In chapter 2, Stuart Langton distinguished between citizen action, which is citizen-initiated and includes bottom-up grassroots groups, and citizen involvement, which is government-initiated and mandated from the top down. Both are supposedly mechanisms to gain power through participation. It is important to point out, however, the unfortunate paradox of our system: that only those at the lower end of the social hierarchy *need* to participate in order to generate power. Large corporate and banking interests, for example, have ample power without any "participation." They are generally able to promote their self-interest successfully through the use of corporate resources and without the sacrifice of much personal time or energy to hearings, meetings, or demonstrations. Individual citizens, on the other hand, are often asked to participate at considerable personal sacrifice in public hearings or on local boards, only to find themselves as powerless as before. The citizen-action approach, then, is based on a substitution of numbers for monetary resources and of commitment and courage for position and authority.

If previous studies and the history described in other essays of this book have anything to tell us, it is that only an active, well-organized group with its own positive agenda and the ability to mobilize people and resources independently can successfully change the way decisions are made or benefits are allocated in our society.

As Sherry Arnstein concluded in her well-known article on citizen participation, "In most cases where power has come to be shared it was *taken* by the citizens, not *given*." She went on to say:

Partnership can work most effectively when there is an organized power-base in the community to which the citizen leaders are accountable; when the citizen group has the financial resources to pay its leaders reasonable honoraria for their time-consuming efforts, and when the group has the resources to hire (and fire) its own technicians, lawyers and community organizers.[1]

Since all of these elements are lacking in governmentally mandated citizen involvement, it is not surprising that even as objective a work as the *Encyclopedia of Social Work* concludes that "in general, citizen participation has not been an effective means of achieving social reform."[2] It cites as evidence Roland Warren's study of 54 agencies involving citizen participation in 6 cities. Although citizens achieved 606 cases of "innovation," they had little impact on agency programs because 559 of these involved superficial modifications of organizational structure or procedures.[3]

Thus, it becomes even more imperative to examine and understand the evolution of the new grassroots movement and explore its potential as a meaningful form of citizen action toward the redistribution of power and wealth in this society.

How Many Grassroots Groups Are There?

Although the total number of grassroots groups or the memberships they reach are virtually impossible to estimate, a few figures may be useful in providing a sense of magnitude.

First, there are some gross estimates of the number of voluntary associations and volunteers in America today. The Alliance for Volunteerism estimates six million voluntary associations (1975), and a study by ACTION indicates thirty-seven million volunteers, or one-fourth of all Americans over the age of 13 (1974).

Attempting to identify those voluntary associations that are neighborhood-based, the National Commission on Neighborhoods recently compiled a list of about 8,000 groups, and HUD's new Office on Neighborhoods, Voluntary Associations, and Consumer Affairs has begun a clearinghouse with 4,000 groups thus far.

The range in the scope of grassroot groups complicates such estimates considerably. It hardly makes sense to count a block club of a few dozen members as a group on a par with a multistate coalition of tens of thousands of members. In a field study of grassroots groups conducted in 1976, the author identified at least three multistate organizations, a dozen city-wide alliances, and thousands of neighborhood associations.[4] Given that there are some 10,000 block clubs in New York City alone, the national estimates would be astronomical. In addition, these groups are expanding at an overwhelming rate. For example:

1. ACORN (Association of Community Organizations for Reform Now) was operating in five states two years ago, at the time of the author's study, and is now in thirteen states with plans to be in two more by December 1978.
2. In 1976, National People's Action had chapters in 104 cities in 30 states and a mailing list of 1,000, and now operates in 116 cities in almost every state of the Union, with 38,000 people on its contact list.
3. Massachusetts Fair Share in 1976 had eight affiliate groups around Boston, with 600 members, and now has 25 groups across the state, with over 13,000 members.

Finally, rather than being limited to certain types of people or neighborhoods, the potential for these groups appears almost unbounded. A recently released Gallup survey sponsored by the Charles F. Kettering and Stuart Mott Foundations (March 1978) shows that a vast majority of urban residents—including a majority of those who wanted to leave their neighborhoods—say they would be willing to volunteer their time and efforts to help solve problems at the neighborhood level. Eighty-nine percent of city dwellers said they would be willing to participate in such activities as signing petitions, attending meetings, writing letters, picketing, and making financial contributions. In fact, 52 percent claimed to have done so already. The study did not specify whether the person was a member of a community organization, but did show that over the past five years, 21 percent had attended at least one meeting concerning a threat to their neighborhood, and 53 percent said they would be willing to do so; and 9 percent had served on a neighborhood committee, with 36 percent saying they would be willing to do so.[5] Even if only half of these people belong to grassroots groups of some kind, the numbers would be astonishing.

The Evolving Sophistication of the Grassroots Groups

As grassroots groups mature, many tend to evolve from single-issue to multi-issue involvement and from "protest to program." Table 6-1 describes the characteristics of the two major types of grassroots groups as observed in 1976: (1) issue-oriented/direct-action groups, and (2) self-help/ alternative institutions. What has happened since then is that many of the more successful groups have combined the two approaches.[6] As Leon Finney of the Woodlawn Organization (TWO) in Chicago describes it, groups

Table 6-1
Comparison of Direction-Action Groups and Alternative Institutions

	Issue-Oriented/Direct-Action	*Self-Help/Alternative Institution*
Age	Most began after 1972; many after 1975	Most began in late 1960s or early 1970s
	Life span generally five years	Many now in second stage of life cycle of "protest to program"
Origins	Alinsky tradition	Civil rights and labor movement origins for community development corporations that began in protest style
	Welfare rights and student movement	War on poverty, model cities, and minority capitalism origins for service delivery and economic development component
		Tenants and coop movement has indigenous origins
Constituency		
Class	"Mass base" of low- and moderate-income people	Predominantly low-income base, with middle-income leadership
Race	Working-class whites and racial minorities united on same side of issues	Mostly black and latino, with some new white ethnic groups
Leadership	Leaders are better educated, younger, more often male, and from higher class background than base	Leaders are better educated, younger, more often male, and from higher class background than base
	Distinction between paid organizer (and staff) and local leaders (and board) on question of accountability	Problem of charismatic founder not being best institutional administrator has led to organizational splits
	Secondary leadership often weak	Secondary leadership often weak
Size		
Membership	Range from tenants union of six members to block clubs of dozens to neighborhood organization of hundreds to state-wide coalition of thousands to multi-state organizations with tens of thousands	Range from no membership at all to 115 affiliate organizations to 14 counties (with 12,000 members) to 120 coops (with 3,000 families)
Staff	Staff size ranges from 1 to 50	Staff size ranges from 10 to 500
Funding	Church contributions	Private foundations, primarily the Ford Foundation
	Membership dues by individuals or associated groups	
	Local fund-raising (bake sales, fairs, picnics, dances, etc.)	Government, primarily through CSA, but increasingly through HUD, Labor, (CETA), Commerce (EDA, OMBE), and Justice (LEAA)

Table 6-1 (cont.)

	Issue-Oriented/Direct-Action	Self-Help/Alternative Institution
Funding (cont.)	Foundations (Stern Fund, John Hay Whitney, Rockefeller Brothers, Laras, New World Foundation, D.J.B. Norman, etc.) Door-to-door canvassing	
Issues	Redlining, tenants' rights, neighborhood preservation, utility-rate structure, property-tax assessments, transportation, budget monitoring, generic drugs, zoning and land use, crime and safety, senior citizens, environmental quality, plant siting and location, commercial revitalization, etc.	Appropriate technology, provision of services, manpower training, economic development, land acquisition and development; provision of credit, construction, large-scale planning, technical assistance, commercial revitalization, etc.
Achievements	Growing astronomically; increased memberships, new chapters and new groups	Leadership development
	Specific victories mounting up toward increased equity and accountability	More and better local service delivery
	Issues clarified, power structure understood, sense of collective competence felt, leadership skills developed	Economic development and job creation, though small, can help improve neighborhood image
Problems	People become "burned out"	Loss of membership base and participatory structure; lack of accountability or community control
	Local victories can't sustain interest	New forms of dependency
	Increasing scope takes best leadership to top levels	Incompatibility of private profit and public welfare
Ideology	Reformist: want to make system work better for the little guy	Reformist: want to make system work better for the little guy
	Generally progressive, pluralist, and populist	Local self-reliance, decentralization, small-is-beautiful mentality
	Tend to anticorporate, anti-bureaucratic sentiments	Sometimes adopt entrepreneurial mentality
	Membership more conservative than leadership	Membership more conservative than leadership
Media Profile	Cultivate good relations with the working press; use the media	Generally seek low profile

go through a cycle of four stages: (1) credibility; (2) representation; (3) negotiation; and (4) institutionalization. They gain initial credibility through winning a victory on an issue of immediate concern to their constituency; and with the potential clout of their members, they negotiate or bargain for further gains on other issues. Then, often to meet the needs of their constituents even further, they begin to deliver direct services and job opportunities, frequently through local economic development or self-help technologies. This institutionalization can only remain viable if the cycle is repeated from the start, with increased credibility, a wider base of representation, and so on.

The grassroots groups of today are increasingly sophisticated in this evolutionary process—and in all the possible combinations and permutations thereof. What makes them uniquely effective in comparison with their predecessors is not only this maturation process but a number of key components that have gone along with that. These are shown in table 6-2.

The single most important factor accounting for the differential effectiveness of grassroots groups is the presence of a full-time, paid, professional staff. There is no way that groups relying entirely on voluntary labor can compete successfully in the complex arena of power politics. And it is this need that raises the issue of fund-raising to critical importance. A recent book describes the various techniques used by grassroots groups, from dues and discounts to potlucks; from direct mail to canvassing; and from concerts to corporate donations.[7]

The second most important factor is the ability to relate local issues to national ones and to maintain active organizations at the community level

Table 6-2
Characteristics of Successful Grassroots Groups

---

1. Full-time, paid, professional staff

2. Well-developed fund-raising capacity

3. Sophisticated mode of operation, including:
   a. Neighborhood street organizing
   b. Advanced issue-research capacity
   c. Information dissemination and exposé techniques
   d. Negotiation and confrontation skills
   e. Management capability in the service delivery and economic development areas
   f. Policy and planning skills
   g. Lobbying skills
   h. Experience in monitoring and evaluating government programs

4. Issue growth from the neighborhood to the nation

5. A support network of umbrella groups, technical assistants, action-research projects, organizer-training schools

6. Expanding coalition building with one another, with public-interest groups, and with labor

---

while building toward a national political force. A recent publication of the National Training and Information Center in Chicago stated:

As the debate has grown, so have the issues. From being denied a $3,000 home improvement loan to the net losses of banks on Real Estate Investment Trusts (REITs) and speculative foreign loans. From that abandoned building on this block to HUD's inability to regulate mortgage bankers. From the home burglary last night to the allocation of funds for the criminal justice system. From an increase in this month's utility bill to fighting the deregulation of the energy industry. From streets and sidewalks in disrepair to how the overall Community Development Act is implemented. The 1970's have seen community organizing go from block issues to federal policy and back again. From testifying against pro-industry legislation on Capitol Hill on getting stray dogs picked up.[8]

The growth of an array of support networks for grassroots organizations is both an indicator of the new level of sophistication and professionalism and a contributing factor to it. The umbrella organizations, clearinghouses, action-research projects, resources, and organizer-training schools help to develop issues, devise strategies, train organizers and leaders, devise policy, promote fund-raising, recruit staff, and facilitate communications between the groups and their constituencies and among the groups themselves. Many groups have newsletters, which aid in this sharing of experience and provide guidelines in plain English to the new federal programs of interest to community groups, debate issues of community concern, advertise conferences and meetings of interest, and list job openings for organizers. Table 6-3 lists some of the support networks and organizer-training schools, with the names of their newsletters and addresses.

Perhaps the most surprising development in the past two years has been the increase in coalitions among grassroots groups, and between them and public-interest and labor organizations. Given the strong egos of many of the organizers, the territorial imperatives of "turf," and the competing organizing philosophies, it was an open question whether such coalitions would be possible. A mutual and increasing recognition of the need for an ever-broader constituent base, new leadership, and the value of merged skills for common goals has led to such new alliances as the Citizen Labor Energy Coalition. This group met 150 strong in Washington on April 20, 1978, as the first joint national merger of community groups, labor, and a public-interest environmental organization. It was chaired by Bill Winpisinger, president of the International Association of Machinists, and included the United Auto Workers, the American Federation of State, County, and Municipal Employees; the Oil, Chemical and Atomic Workers; the Machinists; Steel Workers, and Sheet Metal Workers.

In a similar vein, the Ohio Public Interest Campaign, which is fighting for public accountability of corporations, is composed of affiliatory groups from labor unions, senior-citizen clubs, neighborhood groups, churches,

Table 6-3
Support Networks, Newsletters, and Organizer-Training Schools

Support Network	Address	Name of Newsletter
Center for Community Change (CCC)	1000 Wisconsin Ave., N.W. Washington, D.C. 20007	"Monitor"
Center for Community Economic Development (CCED)	639 Massachusetts Ave. Cambridge, Mass. 02139	"The Center for Community Economic Development Newsletter"
Center for Governmental Studies	P.O. Box 34481 Washington, D.C. 20034	"Neighborhood Ideas"
Institute for Local Self-Reliance	1717 18th St., N.W. Washington, D.C. 20009	"Self-Reliance"
Movement for Economic Justice Education and Training Center (MEJETC)	1735 T St., N.W. Washington, D.C. 20009	"Just Economics"
National Association of Neighborhoods (NAN)	1612 20th St., N.W. Washington, D.C. 20009	"The NAN Bulletin"
National Center for Urban Ethnic Affairs (NCUEA)	1521 16th St., N.W. Washington, D.C. 20036	"National Neighborhood News Service"
National Center for Voluntary Action (NCVA)	1214 16th St., N.W. Washington, D.C. 20036	"Volunteering"
Conference/Alternative State and Local Policies	1901 Q St., N.W. Washington, D.C. 20009	"Ways and Means"
National Congress for Community Economic Development (NCCED)	1029 Vermont Ave., N.W. Washington, D.C. 20036	"Interchange"
National Congress of Neighborhood Women	11-29 Catherine St. Brooklyn, N.Y. 11211	"Neighborhood Women"
National Council of La Raza (NCLA)	1725 Eye St., N.W. Washington, D.C. 20006	"AGENDA: A Journal of Hispanic Issues" (bi-monthly)
National Neighbors, Inc.	815 15th St., N.W. Washington, D.C. 20005	"National Neighbors"

Table 6-3 (cont.)
Support Networks, Newsletters, and Organizer-Training Schools

Support Network	Address	Name of Newsletter
National People's Action (NPA)	1123 West Washington Blvd. Chicago, Ill. 60607	"Disclosure"
National Self-Help Clearinghouse	33 West 42nd St., Rm. 1227 New York, N.Y. 10036	"Self-Help Reporter"
National Self-Help Resource Center, Inc.	2000 S St., N.W. Washington, D.C. 20009	"Network Notes"

Organizer-Training Schools	Address	
Center for Urban Encounter (CUE)	3410 University Ave., S.E. Minneapolis, Minn. 55414	
Industrial Areas Foundation (IAF)	12 E. Grand Avenue Chicago, Ill. 60610	
Mid-American Institute	9401 S. Leavitt Street Chicago, Ill. 60620	
Mid-Atlantic Center for Community Concern	388 Sackett St. Brooklyn, N.Y. 11231	
Midwest Academy	600 W. Fullerton Chicago, Ill. 60614	
National Center for Urban Ethnic Affairs (NCUEA)	1521 16th St., N.W. Washington, D.C. 20036	
National Training and Information Center	1123 W. Washington Blvd. Chicago, Ill. 60607	
New England Training Center for Community Organizers (NETCCO)	19 Davis Street Providence, R.I. 02908	
Organize, Inc.	814 Mission San Francisco, Calif. 94103	
Pacific Institute for Community Organization	3914 E. 14th St. Oakland, Calif. 94601	
The Institute	628 Baronne New Orleans, La. 70113	

minority organizations, and environmental associations. And Connecticut Citizen Action Group, which began as a Nader organization, became a membership direct-action group and now has UAW backing on all of its state-wide issues.

There is no doubt that these coalitions provide added clout and staying power for the entire movement. Massachusetts Fair Share, for example, using the expose tactics of the public-interest movement, was able to get tens of millions of dollars of unpaid corporate taxes back into city coffers and $55 million of overcharges on auto insurance repaid to unfairly charged consumers.

What Have Grassroots Groups Achieved?

The specific achievements of the groups are as varied as their styles, constituents, and locations. They range from legislative victories to neighborhood revitalization, to rural development, to self-help technology. Table 6-4 provides some selected examples.

Table 6-4
Selected Achievements of Grassroots Groups

1. *The New Jersey Federation of Senior Citizens,* since its start in 1975 with a "Rally Against Inflation," has organized 470 groups into a state-wide coalition. Working together, they lobbied successfully for the passage of 11 pieces of state legislation concerning taxes, utility rates, health, and supplemental income, in some cases over the opposition of both industry and labor.

2. In St. Louis, in an all-black neighborhood that many had considered beyond restoration, the *Jeff-Vander-Lou Community Development Corporation* (without any federal money) has rehabilitated 331 housing units, constructed 75 new apartments, and is now working on a 100-unit elderly project and 170 units of infill and scatter sites. It also operates an extensive list of human service programs, has persuaded the construction unions to run an apprenticeship program (which has trained 1,000 people), has attracted a new Brown Shoe Company factory (with 450 jobs) into their area, is redeveloping a deteriorated commercial street into a shopping center, is producing a self-sustaining monthly newspaper called "Proud," and has assembled a blanket insurance plan whereby six insurance companies have combined to provide full home and commercial policies to the neighborhood.

3. *National People's Action* groups, acting at the national level through the Home Mortgage Disclosure Act in December 1975, lobbied successfully for an amendment to the Housing and Community Development Act that reimburses homebuyers for defects in FHA housing, and was instrumental in establishing the Urban Reinvestment Task Force as a separate entity, over HUD's opposition.

4. *MACE (Mississippi Action for Community Education),* active in 14 rural counties of the Mississippi Delta, has succeeded in maintaining an active organizer-training program and voter-registration arm, as well as delivering an array of direct services and providing jobs through their community economic development activities. They are operating a blue jeans factory, Fine Vines, with its own retail store; a number of low-income housing projects; four supermarkets and an agricultural coop. They have elected numerous black officials to local office; and they publish a newspaper called "The Voice of Shrimph."

Table 6-4 (cont.)

5. *U-HAB (Urban Homesteading Assistance Board)* in New York City has taken two problems—housing abandonment and unemployment—and parlayed them into a solution. Using "sweat equity," they rehabilitated vacant or deteriorated housing units. So far, 1,000 units have been rehabilitated, while many useful skills have been taught, small spin-off jobs and businesses have been created, and energy conservation has been promoted.

6. *The People's Development Corporation,* in the South Bronx, in addition to rehabilitating 28 apartments and several community rooms of an abandoned tenement, created a small park, formed a food cooperative, built a solar greenhouse, and set up a group to train others in the skills they had learned.

Each accomplishment and each victory may not be earth-shattering, but as the groups begin to build incrementally on their past achievements, the cumulative picture becomes increasingly impressive. Even in cases where the achievements are reversed or overturned, the experience of involvement remains a valuable one. More and more people are beginning to understand the issues, to see how power and politics operate, to grasp both the potentials and limitations of collective action, and to feel a new sense of self-esteem. Leaders are being created, skills are being developed, and passivity is being challenged.

The Government Response

One indicator of the achievements of the grassroots groups is the new degree of recognition and legitimacy they have been awarded by the national government. President Carter's recently announced national urban policy included "neighborhood groups and voluntary associations," along with all levels of government and the private sector in his "New Partnership to Conserve America's Communities." It allocated $100 million for neighborhoods, which included mini-grants directly to neighborhood organizations (with mayoral concurrence), consumer-cooperative credit unions, an urban volunteer program, community-based crime prevention, a neighborhood arts program, and new resources for neighborhood housing and commercial revitalization.

Even before that, the neighborhood movement had officially come of age with the presidentially-appointed National Commission on Neighborhoods. The National Neighborhoods Policy Act, passed by Congress in 1976 to establish the Commission, grew directly out of efforts by grassroots coalitions throughout the United States. One of its clear mandates was to evaluate citizen-initiated neighborhood revitalization efforts and determine how public policy can best support such efforts.

In the bureaucracy, as well, room is being made for neighborhood groups. HUD has just created a new Office on Neighborhoods, Voluntary Action, and Consumer Affairs (headed by Monsignor Geno Baroni, former director of the National Center for Urban and Ethnic Affairs). ACTION has just created a new office of Volunteerism and Citizen Participation. Even at the city level, the growing importance of citizen-initiated grassroots groups is being recognized, and many city governments are decentralizing their functions and responsibilities so as to devolve power to local community groups and neighborhood agencies. For example, in 1974 Portland, Oregon, adopted an ordinance that allowed the city council to recognize neighborhood organizations that met criteria of open membership. The ordinance established an Office of Neighborhood Associations, with one central and five neighborhood offices, the staff of each being hired by the neighborhood associations, with the consent of the local council member. These offices have a responsibility to notify neighborhood associations of pending measures affecting their neighborhood, to conduct needs assessments, and to gain input into the city's budget process. In Pittsburgh, Pennsylvania, the planning department created a Community Planning Division in 1971, assigning planners to designated neighborhoods with the power, along with community groups, to recommend how the entire capital budget and community development block-grant money should be allocated throughout the city's neighborhoods. The Pittsburgh city charter also allows for the development of elected community advisory boards. In Baltimore, Maryland, a portion of community development block-grant money is channeled directly to community organizations for the purpose of hiring staff and obtaining office space. Even in New York City, after recent charter revisions, there is a move toward more decentralized administration and local planning.

The question then becomes whether this official recognition will "enable" or "disable" the grassroots groups. Will it be another case of "the helping hand strikes again"? Since very often the powerful thing about these groups is their localism, diversity, and autonomy, will governmental recognition, programmatic responsibility, and federal funding be the proverbial kiss of death? Even if co-optation or social control is *not* the government's intent, empowerment is unlikely to be the result.

However, there certainly are measures that government can take to increase the capacity and effectiveness of grassroots groups; for instance, opening up access to information and to the decision-making processes; facilitating peer training and intergroup contacts and communication; providing financial and technical support directly to the groups and indirectly to those mayors who take major steps toward devolving power and decentralizing control down to the neighborhood level; and building participation criteria into federal programs. Some examples are shown in table 6-5.

The transfer of any responsibility to the grassroots level must be accompanied by a transfer of power and control. Decentralized administration without authority is merely a more subtle form of centralized power. Further considerable sensitivity is needed to capitalize upon the strengths of grassroots groups so as to permit them to preserve their integrity while integrating them with the functioning of existing institutions.

The Challenge Ahead

No matter how sophisticated and successful the grassroots movement is, or how sensitive government is in exploiting its potential, there are severe limits to what it can achieve. First, many of the most important decisions and events shaping the lives of community people are determined well beyond the sphere of the neighborhood, often at the national level or even at the international level. Second, many of these decisions are made not by government but by private businesses and banks, which lack even limited accountability to the people affected by their decisions. Steps taken by OPEC and the energy industry or by multinational corporations can affect

Table 6-5
Government Measures for Building Grassroots Capacity

1. Providing access to information and decision making
   a. Disaggregate census data to the neighborhood level and disseminate them to grassroots groups upon request
   b. Notify neighborhood groups in advance of major federal, state, or local activities that would directly affect their interests
   c. Withold federal funds from localities that are not in compliance with citizen participation guidelines at all stages of planning, implementation, and monitoring
   d. Empower community groups to function as independent monitors and evaluators of federal programs

2. Facilitating exchange of experience among grassroots groups
   a. Hold regional conferences on specific issue areas for groups working at the local level
   b. Provide support to the umbrella agencies and resource centers that have been serving the needs of grassroots groups and helping to start new ones
   c. Make available funds for community leaders to visit one another's organizations and to develop and participate in mutual training programs

3. Supporting grassroots groups and decentralization experiments
   a. Provide direct grants (without mayoral concurrence) to groups for staff support, hiring technical assistance, expanding their outreach capacity, or developing a project or program that meets local needs (either as a parallel activity or as replacement of government funds)
   b. Conduct public-relations campaigns through the mass media, stressing the legitimacy and value of grassroots activity, self-help, and volunteerism

the quality of life of neighborhood people far more profoundly than a fair-share utility bill or a campaign against corporate tax abatement.

As the locus of decisions shifts from neighborhood to nation, from national to international, and from public to private, the challenge to the grassroots movement is ever greater. The groups must make the link between the macro-issues of the day and the micro-events of their own lives; they must begin to organize for the social accountability of nongovernmental institutions; and they must contrive to build their organizational strength simultaneously at the community and the national level. No one but themselves has the will or the capacity to act on their own behalf.
behalf.

Whether or not it is possible to meet this challenge, and whether the grassroots initiatives will ultimately serve to lubricate the wheels of the system or to create the seeds of significant social transformation, are open questions. But what seems clear is that, in either case, the survival, growth, and independence of the grassroots groups—not individually, but as a movement—are critical to the survival of our democracy.

As President John F. Kennedy once said, "Those who make peaceful revolutions impossible make violent revolutions inevitable."

It is precisely the making of peaceful revolutions that is the business of the grassroots groups in the United States today.

Notes

1. Sherry Arnstein, "A Ladder of Citizen Participation," *Journal of the American Institute of Planners* 35 (July 1969):221.

2. Peggy Wireman, "Citizen Participation," in *The Encyclopedia of Social Work* (Washington: National Association of Social Workers, 1977), pp. 175-180.

3. Roland Warren, *The Structure of Urban Reform,* (Lexington, Mass.: Lexington Books, D.C. Heath and Company, 1974).

4. Janice E. Perlman, "Grassrooting the System," *Social Policy* 7 (1976).

5. George Gallup, "Strong Neighborhoods Offer Hope for the Nation's Citizen," *The Gallup Poll* (March 5, 1978).

6. For some excellent case studies of this evolution, see Hans Spiegel, *From Protest to Program: Three Grassroots Coalitions in Their Formative Stages* (New York: Hunter College, April 1978).

7. Cf. Joan Flanagan, *The Grassroots Fundraising Book: How to Raise Money in your Community* (Chicago: The Swallow Press, Inc., 1977).

8. *Neighborhoods First: From the '70s into the '80s* (Chicago: National Training and Information Center, 1977), p. 4.

7

Public Involvement as Reform and Ritual: The Development of Federal Participation Programs

Walter A. Rosenbaum

In little more than a decade we have witnessed a radical redefinition of public rights in the federal administrative process. The "new" public involvement arrived as a few precarious innovations during the 1960s. By the late 1970s, this innovation threatened to become a cliche as a multitude of statutory mandates and agency regulations, most minted in recent years, prescribed citizen involvement in agency affairs vastly exceeding the standard once considered appropriate. Such programs continue to proliferate in number and substantive detail, yet this seems in many respects a counterfeit prosperity. Few programs apparently have worked well. Some are rituals; many are moribund. Why, despite admirable intent and years of dedicated effort by reformers, do such schemes often falter badly in implementation? One reason apparently lies in the history of program advocacy.

The new programs have often been promoted on the basis of inarticulate or untested assumptions about appropriate goals and procedures. These strategic theories have seldom been critically examined. It will be helpful to describe briefly the evolution of the new programs with special attention to the adequacy of several key concepts undergirding program development. This raises unsettling but productive questions about the credibility of such theory; it points toward reevaluation and reformulation of program design. In essence, we can regard the history of existing programs as a valuable "laboratory" in which the sturdiness of program ideas has been tested by experience.

Public Involvement: Old, Newer, Newest

The "new" public involvement consists of two general programs largely developed during the last two decades and a newer experiment instituted in 1977. Together they depart significantly from traditional standards for public involvement prevailing in federal agency affairs until the early 1960s.

The Traditional Standard

The familiar standard for public involvement in federal agencies was the Administrative Procedures Act (APA)—conservative, constraining upon the public, but broadly understood and seldom controversial into the 1960s.[1] The APA customarily required only that an agency provide for public notice and comment during rule making, offer opportunities for group representation during trial-type hearings ("adjudications") or during quasi-judicial rule making "on the record," and when appropriate, hold public hearings, at its discretion, on other matters. The Freedom of Information Act and its recent amendments, in addition, require that all governmental agencies, upon request, provide the public with papers, opinions, records, policy statements, and staff manuals.[2] These approaches reflected a common philosophy: responsibility for initiating involvement largely rested with the public; involvement was to be confined to specified forms at limited points in administrative proceedings (usually late in policy development); and the public was left to its own resources in attempting to apprehend the substance and procedure attending important decisions. In effect, if not by intent, it confined the mobilized public largely to middle- and upper-class organized interests able to obtain the legal counsel usually required for effective intervention under these conditions.

Mobilizing the Underprivileged

Then came the Economic Opportunity Act (1964), with its unprecedented congressional mandate, at once nebulous and controversial, that the Office of Economic Opportunity (OEO) achieve "maximum feasible participation" among the poor in its community action programs.[3] Two years later, the Demonstration Cities and Metropolitan Development Act (1966) insisted that HUD create "widespread" participation among those affected by program grants.[4] The OEO and HUD programs departed substantially from the traditional APA approach to participation: agencies apparently were obliged to encourage involvement among "target" populations of the poor. OEO and HUD officials treated these mandates as an invitation to mobilize the poor aggressively for active involvement in community allocation of program grants, although the underprivileged are traditionally weak in organizational resources and participatory skills. This, in fact, considerably exceeded the apparent congressional intent in writing these participation mandates. Sponsors of the OEO legislation, for instance, thought of "maximum feasible participation" largely as "a nice sentiment and a means of giving the administrator of the program power to prevent segregation of community action programs."[5] Writers of the HUD participation mandate, seeking to avoid the "excesses" Congress perceived in the earlier

OEO program, shunned any encouragement to mobilize the underprivileged for extensive involvement in program implementation. Both participation programs were subsequently suffocated under controversy and criticism arising, in good part, from the unanticipated impact of the poor's involvement in program development.[6] Nevertheless, an important principle had been established. Congress in effect "recognized the vested interest and certain corollary of unspecified rights of the people who are directly affected by public programs"—participation was now a right rather than a privilege.[7]

Mobilizing Diffuse Publics

The newest wave of federal participation programs, by far the most numerous, apply this assumption of a participation right in a different manner. Essentially, these programs retain the concept of affirmative agency responsibility to encourage public involvement in programs without usually specifying a "target" population. The concept abandons the standard of "maximum" or "widespread" participation, but retains an implied assumption that most aspects of agency planning are—at least theoretically—open to public involvement. These new programs affect a potentially vast range of middle- to upper-class groups, because programs largely public in nature are commonly involved (as distinguished from the OEO and HUD legislation aimed specifically at the poor). The programs imply public involvement at many stages of policy planning through many techniques, and thus procedures are presumably open-ended in method and administrative locus. Further, the operational meaning of new involvement strategies is largely unspecified by law, and consequently agencies are invested with considerable discretion in implementation.

The prototype of these new programs can be found in Sec. 101(e) of the Federal Water Pollution Control Act Amendments (FWPCAA) of 1972:

Public participation in the development, revision and enforcement of any regulation, standard, effluent limitation, plan or program established by the Administrator, or any State under this Act shall be provided for, encouraged and assisted by the Administrator and the states. . . .[8]

Other similar provisions for public involvement have now been created, by congressional enactment or agency regulation, so energetically that they are becoming a new federal house style. The rapid proliferation of these broad, vague involvement mandates is suggested by the summary in table 7-1, based upon materials found in a guide to federal participation programs recently published by the U.S. Community Services Administration. The multiplication of involvement programs generally, and those aimed at diffuse publics especially (Type III in table 7-1), are suggested by a few summary statistics:

Table 7-1
Federal Public-Participation Programs, by Type and Date of Creation

Type of Program	Before 1964	1964/5	1966/7	1968/9	1970/1	1972/3	1974/5	1976/7	Total
I. Participation confined only, or primarily, to advisory committees	17	16	6	11	12	28	6	—	96
II. Participation confined only, or primarily, to public meetings and notice	6	—	—	6	3	18	5	—	38
III. Participation implicitly or explicitly permits a broad range of modes, locations, and publics within agency activities	4	3	1	—	6	26	6	16	62
IV. Participation procedures vague or unspecified	9	10	—	—	2	9	—	—	30
Total	36	29	7	17	23	81	17	16	226

Source: U.S. Federal Regional Council, Community Services Administration, *Citizen Participation* (January 1, 1978)

1. Sixty-one percent of all the public-participation programs (137 of 226) were created during or after 1970.
2. Eighty-seven percent of the Type III programs were created during or after 1970.
3. The proportion of all participation programs aimed at a general public and involving open-ended means has increased steadily in recent years; in 1968-1969 there were none, but in the succeeding two-year intervals through 1977 proportions were 26 percent, 32 percent, 35 percent, and 100 percent.

Letting the Sunshine In

In 1977, Congress wrote the "Government in the Sunshine Act," which required about 50 federal boards, commissions, and other agencies with two or more heads or directors to open their meetings to public observation.[9] While numerous exceptions to public scrutiny are permitted, the affected agencies are required to keep transcripts of proceedings available in case of litigation. The law, whose primary impact is upon federal regulatory commissions, also prevents informal, *ex parte* communication between agency officials and representatives of institutions with which the agencies conduct business. While the law appears to expand the range of federal agency procedures to which the public has a right of access, it is closer to earlier APA and Freedom of Information Act philosophies in placing the responsibility for initiating the sustaining involvement upon the affected publics. This legislation is so new that evaluations have yet to be conducted.

The advocacy of the newest participation programs aimed at diffuse publics has been inspired by a number of suppositions, largely implicit, about the causes and consequences of public involvement. These, the theoretical bedrock upon which an elaborate structure of program expectations has been erected, merit brief description.

Some Crucial Theories

"Policies imply theories."[10] At best, the theories in the usual literature on public involvement are inarticulate presumptions, lacking clarity. The literature of public participation is commonly one of advocacy and exhortation; one is expected to read and believe. Writes one exponent: "The question to be asked is not *whether* but *how* to involve the public." Apparently, *if* the public can be involved in programs as described, *if* prescribed procedures work, and *when* programs work are irrelevant.[11] Thus, Norman Wengert's summary of public-participation literature in recent decades seems just: "Enthralled with moralisms and hortatory stances, many who have written on the subject have not undertaken the analysis, nor the empirical work necessary to support their many premises."[12] These theories have been more elaborately analyzed elsewhere; following is a summary review.[13]

The Administrative Devil Theory

It has been almost axiomatic in the literature of the new participation that a major impediment to broad and effective public involvement in administrative procedure—perhaps the major obstacle—is bureaucratic resistance. In ways elegant, blunt, and brutal, bureaucrats are commonly blamed in participation literature for thwarting public involvement in agency proceedings. Motivations commonly cited for this resistance constitute a dismal catalog of administrative delinquency: administrators are variously indicted as secretive, self-serving, nonimaginative, "susceptible to functional lying," deceitful, conservative, locked into a "planning mentality," professionally arrogant, politically protective of agency and career interests, parochial, and lazy.[14] Given such varied explanations for feeble administrative sensitivity to public viewpoints and the fact that perhaps 80 percent to 90 percent of agency decisions were not formally reviewable by the public under APA procedures, it is understandable that reformers should want greater public oversight of agencies. Small wonder, too, that a choir of commentators presumes that public involvement will be likely to prosper if only bureaucrats can be persuaded, or badgered, into including the public in agency activities.

The Pluralist Imperative

Commentators on public participation have commonly asserted that effective participation requires a vigorous pluralism among the interests active in the process; such pluralism can be, and should be, a primary program goal. In developing this argument, certain corollaries are usually added: (1) agencies have a responsibility to promote this diversity of organized groups and viewpoints; and (2) agencies have a special obligation to promote participation by those publics customarily inarticulate and unorganized, yet significantly affected by programs. Behind this confidence in pluralism lies a conviction that the public interest is most likely to emerge from the interplay and conflict between a multitude of interests actively pursuing their own ends at crucial points in policy development.

The Participation Thesis

It is often asserted in participation literature that citizen involvement in governmental programs creates greater citizen social responsibility, promotes civic competence, and encourages willingness to accept programs to which participation is contributed. The value of participation as civic education, according to one analyst, is that the "citizen should gain in knowledge and understanding, develop a deeper sense of social responsibility, and broaden his perspectives beyond the narrow confines of his private life."[15] Administrators may find the participation thesis appealing because it enlists their self-interest by suggesting that what is good for the public is expedient for the agency. It is often asserted in participation literature that broad public involvement is a solvent to dissent because those who are initially unreconciled to government policies came to value the programs they help to shape. Jack Rothman translates this maxim into administrative language:

Only those programs which are determined by citizens will be vigorously carried out. . . . When people take part in determining policies, they will lend themselves to and support those policies in the long run.[16]

The Containment Thesis

Evangelists for the new participation tend to assume, almost routinely, that administrative discretion naturally favors policies advancing agency, professional, or personal administrative fortunes. The administrative process, asserts Joseph Sax, Jr., tends to produce "not the voice of the people but the voice of the bureaucrat."[17] Many commentators favor public involvement because it can reduce administrative freedom to make decisions from narrowly professional bureaucratic or self-interested motivations; it will force broader public concerns on agency consciousness.

So abbreviated a recasting of propositions from participation literature doubtless fails to acknowledge the few sophisticated studies rising above the common level. We have, however, identified some salient arguments for new programs and can proceed to assess actual program accomplishments with these familiar propositions as a standard.

The Fate of Programs

The early fate of EPA's public-involvement mandate in Sec. 101(e) of the FWPCAA ought to be a cautionary tale. Freighted with high expectations by proponents, the program's early history illuminates the general condition of most similar undertakings in recent years. The tale has been told in detail elsewhere.[18] Three years after the program's inception, the National Commission on Water Quality, charged with evaluating the impact of Sec. 101(e), delivered an obituary on its condition in 1975:

> Even in the loosest sense of the term, EPA activities do not constitute a program. There are no explicit objectives; no one is assigned responsibility; there is no direction; there are no funds; there are no plans; there are no obvious attempts to enforce the provisions of the existing regulations.[19]

The EPA has recently sought diligently to exhume and revive its public-involvement activities; evaluations have yet to appear. The early history of the program, however, bears a strong resemblance to the fate of most similar programs that have been evaluated. The EPA can claim not only the prototype program but, unfortunately, prototype results. Generally, findings about many other federal programs seem often to contradict the basic assumptions concerning what participation can or should accomplish.

First, agencies with new participation responsibilities seldom have sought to involve a broad range of individuals in the programs—at least they achieved no such diversity—and agencies rarely have initiated or continued a diversity of procedures to inform groups or individuals about the programs. This was true, of course, even during the OEO and HUD programs. The EPA's participants were drawn almost exclusively from white, middle- to upper-class environmental and public-interest groups.[20] Restricted participation patterns—usually duplicating the social-class bias of the EPA activists—were reported by the General Accounting Office from new citizen-involvement programs in the Federal Aviation Agency and the Federal Highway Administration.[21] The Corps of Engineers, after initiating an imaginative new involvement program with considerable enthusiasm in the early 1970s, largely abandoned it after three years (although it apparently has been revived recently).[22] The National Water Resource Council proposed in early 1975 to create a "Working Group on Public Participation" to provide member agencies with uniform guidance on expanded participation efforts akin to Sec. 101(e). The group met twice briefly and adjourned—permanently and unlamented. The EPA did promote considerable involvement among environmental and public-interest groups in the passage and implementation of the Clean Air Act Amendment through the creation of a "Breather's Lobby" in Washington and the states.[23] But the agency was so unsuccessful in getting the states to meet requirements for adequate public notice before adoption of state pollution control plans that the National Resource Defense Fund reported only five states in substantial compliance.[24]

Second, mandates for public involvement were so customarily brief and vague, and so often unaccompanied by subsequent congressional oversight, as to leave the responsible agencies with enormous discretion in deciding when, how, and where to put them into operation. Legislative histories of participation provisions commonly tell no tales concerning legislative intent; the 1700-page history of the FWPCAA, for instance, contains a single uninstructive sentence on Sec. 101(e).[25] So thin was the characteristic legislative guidance for the new public involvement strategies that the GAO has urged the Office of Management and Budget to take responsibility for developing operational guidelines for such activities.[26] The Advisory Commission on Intergovernmental Relations has asserted that program standards for public involvement have been a major excuse for agency indifference to such mandates at all government levels.[27] The result of this absence in performance standards was to preserve, rather than to constrain, administrative discretion in promoting public-involvement activities.

Finally, it was almost always discovered that public-involvement programs, regardless of details, attract a very limited audience, one that includes (1) representatives of organized interests likely to have been active already in agency affairs; (2) spokesmen for other governmental agencies; and (3) the well-educated, affluent, and politically seasoned. The OEO programs, suggests Irving Lazar, were dominated by "the upwardly mobile, power-seeking, politically ambitious and angry people"; the OEO's Training and Technical Assistance Program, noted another consultant, stimulated involvement not from the typical ghetto resident but "among the relatively few already involved" in political activities.[28] Both the EPA's involvement programs under Sec. 101(e) of the FWPCAA and the Clean Air Act attracted principally environmentalists, public-interest groups, and other middle-class organizations. After reviewing experience with various participation strategies, one proponent of the new involvement was driven to admit "it is an uphill, not to say a losing battle, to engage local publics in debating issues."[29] Even the Corps of Engineers, with the very model of prescribed participation procedures, produced not a vigorous pluralism but a middle-class, educated, politically experienced public, which dominated the program in the early 1970s.

Explaining Program Outcomes

What went wrong with such programs? A number of factors appear to account for these early program failures. Some failures are apparently attributable to poor implementation. But other program problems may have arisen not from the failure of effort or resources, but perhaps from the inadequacy of theories.

The Problem of Compliance Incentives

Most agencies with legislatively mandated or internally created involvement programs made feeble efforts to create organizational prerequisites for their operation. Several explanations seem probable:

1. *Congress, probably deliberately, failed to provide incentives for program implementation.* Congress commonly shows a hearty disinterest in the fate of these programs; it usually fails to clarify program goals or to appropriate significant sums for implementation. Edwin Haefle has noted that legislators shun the politically unrewarding task of mediating between groups when deciding which publics will participate and when and how they will participate in such programs.[30] Rather, Congress ordains the programs to subdue the clamor for expanded participation by bestowing on the agitators a symbolic reward in the form of a nebulous participation mandate, and leaves the bureaucracy—seldom trained for the task—to define ground rules.

2. *Congress often penalized agencies swiftly and painfully when involvement schemes mobilized effective opposition to programs beloved of influential legislators or when new citizen groups, sustained by the program, competed effectively with existing organizations that enjoyed legislative favor.*[31] The moral to this situation was hardly lost on the bureaucracy. Agencies often came to equate vigorous participation programs, with their heightened group conflict, as high-risk situations to be avoided.

3. *Participation programs often promoted goals incompatible with agency objectives and bureaucratic incentives.* Peter Clark and James Q. Wilson have suggested that bureaucracies have tangible and intangible incentives to offer individuals in return for their organizational contribution. For mission-oriented agencies, not only material rewards but "purposes become incentives"—"purposes" in the sense of agency objectives, program goals, and perhaps the opportunity to exercise professional skills.[32] Involvement programs, in effect, often amount to proposals that an agency cultivate criticism of its mission, planning, and professional judgment. Indeed, when social groups that are commonly the least involved in the administrative process do mobilize—especially the disadvantaged—they are often likely to be suspicious of, if not antagonistic to, program goals. (The poor, for instance, may have no reason or reward for accepting environmental programs on any terms.) As Wilson observes, the class composition of a constituency may largely determine its policy viewpoints.[33] Even the active middle-class organizations may enter participation programs enthusiastic about the procedure, yet unreconciled to the sponsoring agency's goals—before or after they have participated in the program.

In brief, bureaucrats may resist the new programs because such arrangements confront conscientious officials with the demand that they adopt attitudes or behaviors at variance with those thought necessary for organizational productivity. Administrative motivation can be considered not as a solution to the problem of achieving public involvement but as a problem in itself. Can incentives for implementing the new involvement plans be compatible with other purposive incentives for the bureaucrat?

The Pluralism Problem

Often, it appears, pluralism failed when programs were conscientiously implemented. Highly restricted participation may be normal and, perhaps, inevitable. In any event, the resources needed to promote a broader pluralism than that usually achieved may have been vastly underestimated and the motivational obstacles to participation too easily ignored.

1. *Many groups and individuals have had no strong incentives to participate in such programs; they may have had strong incentives not to participate.* A number of social theorists have pointed out that individuals likely to obtain some "public good" through programs—and most of the new participation schemes are involved with programs intended to deliver "public goods"—have strong, rational reasons not to participate in organizations working to deliver that good. Mancur Olson has suggested that what is often necessary to get individuals to work in organized activities aimed at obtaining some public good (environmental protection, for instance, or consumer product safety) is some "selective and separate incentive"—that is, some incentive apart from whatever portion of the collective good an individual might obtain whether or not he participates in any organized activity to get it.[34] It is difficult to imagine what selective incentive most environmental programs offer to stimulate latent or apathetic publics to organize and represent themselves. The underprivileged sometimes respond to material incentives, but few participation programs offer such. (A possible selective incentive to encourage, especially, lower-class involvement would be subsidies for group activity.)

2. *Although the administrative cost of producing a vigorous pluralism were likely to be quite high, the actual resources for reaching diffuse publics were commonly limited.* The marginal cost, in dollars and personnel, to add to participation programs new groups beyond those already active is large because additional groups must be sought out vigorously; the programs must be translated into relevant language to them; and generally, such groups must be mobilized rather than simply "informed."

3. *Many agencies probably felt little pressure from those in the programs to expand the range of involved groups, especially when supplemental participants might be antagonistic to those already involved.* The new

participation may actually be creating a new influence structure, which selective interests, already administratively active, have exploited in hope of greater success; one might expect the agency-group relations to stabilize within the structure without producing any strong pressure for greater heterogeneity of participants. Administrators have reason to favor such an arrangement. It precludes a constantly fluid, unpredictable participation pattern in which the behavior of new groups cannot be well anticipated and strategies for accommodating the new participants cannot be made part of the routine.

The Consensus Problem

The frequent failure of the participation thesis should cause proponents of expanded public participation great concern. Contrary to expectations, it often appears that broad public involvement in agency planning did not necessarily (or usually) lead to greater public acceptance of programs and, therefore, greater ease in program accomplishment. While participation might have produced "civic education" and heightened social responsibility among participants, such impacts have been highly elusive to measurement. Of the Army Corps of Engineers' experience with the participation thesis in the early 1970s, Daniel Mazmanian writes:

[W]hile the most extensive public participation efforts have won acclaim and credibility for the agency, they have more often than not failed to build a consensus on the plans that emerge out of the planning process.[35]

In this and other instances of public participation in governmental programs cited by numerous investigators, the values and program loyalties of participants were not especially susceptible to alteration through participation experiences. Thus, participation programs often seem to produce, at best, greater approval of sponsoring agencies for their participation endeavors, but *not* greater program consensus among participants.

The Discretion Problem

Agencies implementing new involvement programs were often left a large amount of freedom to decide what "publics" would be involved, when involvement would occur, and how. Agencies might complain about nebulous program standards, but they often prefer them, for several reasons:

1. *Vague standards allow agencies or subordinate units room to maneuver in dealing with their constituency, the Congress, or other administrative units.* Regional offices of EPA, for example, frequently re-

laxed standards for public notice and hearing, which are required of the states in formulating their funding priorities for waste-treatment plants under the FWPCAA, as a means of bargaining for greater state compliance with other provisions of the law. Such internal agency bargaining over the terms of public involvement was probably common to most programs in the early 1970s.

2. *It is often impossible to reach agreement on the meaning of crucial terms in public-involvement programs.* One can create conflicting and competing definitions of "public participation" or "public involvement." Given the inherent difficulty of defining key terms in involvement programs, it is understandable that legislative guidance and administrative regulations sometimes leave definitions vague or absent. But this situation is paradoxical and possibly pernicious in the light of participation ideologies. Generous administrative discretion permits administrators to ignore some publics and enhance (if unwittingly) the opportunities for administrative access among others. Rather than curbing the arbitrary exercise of administrative discretion in program development, this appears to perpetuate it. Such discretion may not be abused. To the extent it has been, it moves beyond paradox to a parody of reform.

Looking Ahead

The late 1970s appear to mark a second phase in the development of the new public involvement in federal programs. In retrospect, the period from 1960 through 1975 was largely a time during which programs were formally created and initial experiments in their implementation were attempted. Beginning in the late 1970s, the federal government seems to be moving toward an intensified commitment and reassessment of the programs in anticipation of their further growth.

In several respects, the future of the programs seems more robust than their past. For the first time since the early 1960s, the White House appears actively concerned with encouraging expanded participation in administrative procedures. This may be a harbinger of vastly increased fiscal and manpower resources needed by agencies to revive moribund programs and to elevate others beyond ritual and tokenism. Equally important, the formation of the Federal Interagency Council on Citizen Participation, coupled with vigorous early leadership, seems to be fashioning an effective source of program guidance, encouragement, and coordination among the numerous federal agencies with involvement programs. Moreover, several agencies with involvement commitments touching a potentially broad public—especially the EPA and the Corps of Engineers—have recently initiated major program re-evaluations and upgrading.

Renewed program activity, however welcome, can easily become motion without progress unless it is combined with a tough-minded examination of the four theories undergirding so many program structures. This examination should seek to clarify the factors, or combination of factors, that are associated with the attainment of these theoretical ends; or, alternatively, to identify why such theories ought to be revised. This is especially important now, because several federal programs now operating on a massive but short-term scale involve a very interesting range of public-participation strategies and social settings. The EPA's "208 Program" (Areawide Water Quality Management), for instance, embraces 149 water planning agencies now actively attempting to implement the mandate in Sec. 101(e) of the FWPCAA in every state; these agencies will have largely completed their work by the early 1980s. An extremely valuable, perhaps unique, opportunity exists to examine these programs as if they were 149 "laboratories" of public-involvement activity. Careful investigation, firmly grounded conceptually and empirically, might add significantly to our understanding of the conditions under which involvement schemes do or do not work. Similar opportunities appear to exist within the varied programs supervised by the Corps' Institute of Water Resources.

In short, timely, appropriate, and constant program evaluation, intended to test participation ideology and rhetoric by experience, will enhance our ability to interpret the brief but rich history of existing new programs and to design better future programs.

Notes

1. 5 U.S.C. 551.
2. 5 U.S.C. 552.
3. 78 Stat. 508, 202(a)(3) (1964).
4. The concept of "widespread" participation, like "organizing the unorganized," was imputed to the law by HUD officials as a result of their interpretation of legislative intent. The Housing Act of 1954 might be considered the earliest example of "targeted" participation programs, but its participation mandate, as interpreted by federal officials until 1969, largely confined participation to more traditional forms; and in any event, the language of the statute did not suggest involvement of the underprivileged.
5. Sar Levitan, *The Great Society's Poor Law* (Baltimore: Johns Hopkins University Press, 1969), p. 44. For a general discussion of this issue, see Richard L. Cole, *Citizen Participation and the Urban Policy Process* (Lexington, Mass.: Lexington Books, D.C. Heath and Company, 1974), Ch. 1.
6. The fate of the programs is summarized in Daniel P. Moynihan, *Maximum Feasible Misunderstanding* (New York: The Free Press, 1970).

7. Robert C. Seaver, "The Dilemmas of Citizen Participation," in H.B.C. Spiegel, ed., *Citizen Participation in Urban Development* (Washington: Institute for Applied Behavioral Science, 1968), p. 62.

8. 33 U.S.C. 1151.

9. 90 Stat. 1241.

10. Jeffrey L. Pressman and Aaron B. Wildavsky, *Implementation* (Berkeley: University of California Press, 1973), xv. The analysis of participation theory leans heavily on the theoretical preface to this book.

11. Erasmus H. Kloman, "Public Participation in Technology Assessment," *Public Administration Review* 35 (1974):57.

12. Norman Wengert, "Public Participation in Water Planning: A Critique of Theory, Doctrine and Practice," *Water Resources Bulletin* 7 (1971):28. See also Jack Rothman, *Planning and Organizing for Social Change* (New York: Columbia University Press, 1974), p. 282.

13. Walter A. Rosenbaum, "The New Public Participation: A Reappraisal," *Journal of Voluntary Action Research* 8 (1978).

14. See, for example, Advisory Commission on Intergovernmental Relations, *Regional Decision-making: New Strategies for Substate Districts* (Washington: U.S. Government Printing Office, 1973), p. 335; Joseph F. Coates, "Why Public Participation is Essential in Technology Assessment," *Public Administration Review* 78 (1975):67.

15, Jack L. Walker, "A Critique of the Elitist Theory of Democracy," *American Political Science Review* 60 (1966). See also Peter Bachrach, *The Theory of Democratic Elitism* (Boston: Little, Brown, 1978), p. 101.

16. Rothman, *Planning and Organizing*, p. 281.

17. Joseph L. Sax, Jr., *Defending the Environment* (New York: Alfred A. Knopf, 1971).

18. Rothman, *Planning and Organizing*.

19. National Commission on Water Quality, *Assessment of Public Participation in the Implementation of the Federal Water Pollution Control Act Amendments of 1972: Draft Final Report* (Washington: National Commission on Water Quality, 1975), p. 73.

20. Walter A. Rosenbaum, "Slaying Beautiful Hyoptheses with Ugly Facts: EPA and Public Participation," 6 *Journal of Voluntary Action Research* 6 (1978).

21. Comptroller General of the United States, *Public Involvement in Planning Public Works Projects Should be Increased,* Report B-153449 (Washington: U.S. Government Printing Office, 1974).

22. The tale of the Corps' early experience with public involvement is summarized in Daniel A. Mazmanian, "Prospects for Public Participation in Federal Agencies: The Case of the Corps of Engineers," in John C. Pierce and Harvey R. Doerksen, eds., *Water Politics and Public Involvement* (Ann Arbor, Mich.: Ann Arbor Science, 1976), pp. 225-248.

23. 84. Stat. 1626 (1970).

24. U.S. Senate, Committee on Public Works, Subcommittee on Air and Water Pollution, *Implementation of the Clean Air Act of 1970,* Part I, pp. 29-30.

25. U.S. Library of Congress, Congressional Reference Service, *Legislative History of the Federal Water Pollution Control Act Amendments of 1972,* Vols. I and II. Document No. 93-1 (Washington: D.C.: U.S. Government Printing Office, 1973).

26. U.S. Comptroller General, *Public Involvement,* pp. 25-26.

27. Advisory Commission on Intergovernmental Relations, *Regional Decision-making,* p. 209.

28. Irving Lazar, "Which Citizens Should Participate in What?" in E.S. Cahn and B.A. Passett, eds., *Citizen Participation: Effecting Community Change* (New York: Praeger Publishers, 1971), p. 99.

29. Kloman, "Public Participation," p. 57.

30. Edwin Haefle, *Representative Government and Environmental Management* (Baltimore: Johns Hopkins Press, 1973), p. 118.

31. On the EPA experience with such penalties, see Rosenbaum, "Slaying Beautiful Hypotheses with Ugly Facts."

32. Peter B. Clark and James Q. Wilson, "Incentive Systems: A Theory of Organizations," *Administrative Science Quarterly* 6 (1961):129-147.

33. James Q. Wilson, *Political Organizations* (New York: Basic Books, 1973).

34. Mancur Olson, Jr., *The Logic of Collective Action,* (Cambridge, Mass.: Harvard University Press, 1965), p. 51.

35. Daniel B. Mazmanian, "Citizens and the Assessment of Technology," Paper presented at the 1974 Annual Meeting of the American Political Science Association, Chicago, Illinois, August 29-September 2, 1974, p. 4.

8

Implementing Public Involvement Programs in Federal Agencies

Jerry Delli Priscoli

How does an agency of the federal government effectively implement a citizen-involvement program? As a social scientist with responsibilities for citizen-involvement programs in a federal agency, this is a continuing live question for me. In seeking to answer the question, I have found that it is particularly helpful to be aware of three elements: (1) the inherent problems that are common in all attempts to implement citizen involvement; (2) the most common pitfalls of agencies in the implementation process and how they can be avoided or managed; and (3) practical guidelines and questions that make it easier to plan and implement citizen involvement. This essay reflects my personal perspective concerning these three elements as a result of efforts to learn how an effective citizen-involvement program can be implemented by an agency.

Some Inherent Problems in Implementing Citizen-Involvement Programs

Although there are innumerable problems in implementing citizen-involvement programs, I have found that four overriding ones continually surface: coordination, control, representativeness, and dissonance. Although these problems are never "solved," they can and should be creatively managed.

Coordination: One of the most critical problems for government today is the relationship between different governmental units and levels. Often policies and/or plans of one agency are implemented by another. Projects or facilities of one agency may even be operated or maintained by a second, third, and fourth. Furthermore, actions are rarely limited to federal agencies. State, local, and private actors are also involved, and each agency may embody different missions and purposes. As a consequence of this mix of purposes and actors, different citizen-involvement programs frequently are developed. In some cases, these programs ameliorate interagency and citizen-government conflict; in others, they generate such conflict.

Control: When a federal agency deals with a public-policy issue, its responsibility is to find and assure the federal interest. Such interest frequently

97

takes the form of centralized control through regulation, licensing, funding, and the like. Citizen involvement, however, is by nature a decentralizing concept. Therefore, a tension always exists between the centralized needs of the agency and the decentralized interests of citizens. Every citizen-involvement program consequently must confront the question: How much centralized control should the agency apply to assure sufficiently responsive, decentralized citizen involvement?

Representativeness: One of the most frequent criticisms of citizen-involvement programs is that the citizens who become involved don't represent the majority, but rather are a "citizen elite" that represents special interests. This is a very serious problem for agencies that make use of citizen involvement to develop consensus and support for a policy or program. For this reason, agencies must develop multiple links in the citizen involvement process. In so doing, however, it is doubtful that conflict can be avoided. To most agencies with established clients and constituencies and traditional methods of relating to them, a more representative involvement process may be painful, and the process may be aborted to avoid conflict. Unfortunately, this frequently leads to problems of public opposition at a later date.

Dissonance: One of the facts of life for government agencies is the conflict between political interests and technical interests in decision making. The excessive practice of using technical justifications to rationalize controversial political discussions is undoubtedly one of the factors that has led to greater demands for citizen involvement. As a result, government agencies should expect that citizen involvement will increase the tension between technical and political considerations. They cannot avoid the question: To what extent is an agency plan or regulation technically objective or purely political. Since finding workable solutions to blending technical and political dimensions is a critical, internal agency task, citizen involvement will force this issue to the surface and encourage meaningful resolution.

Two Common Pitfalls in Implementing Citizen Involvement

As government agencies seek to cope with the problems inherent in implementing citizen-involvement programs, their efforts frequently falter because of two common pitfalls. The first arises at the stage of writing citizen-involvement regulations, and the second arises in relation to agency routines. In the following pages, I should like to describe the situations in which these pitfalls arise and discuss alternative ways of coping with them.

Writing Citizen-Involvement Regulations: Curing the Disease with More of the Disease

When faced with a mandate, government agencies predictably turn to writing regulations. This is true, too, with citizen involvement. To date, most federal agencies have written specific citizen-involvement regulations. Such agency regulations are useful in many ways. For example, they legitimize discussion of citizen involvement. Professionals at all levels throughout the agency can openly debate the merits and shortcomings of involvement. Managers often are enabled to budget funds and hire new people. Questions of effectiveness and evaluation are raised as programs are designed. In short, a new program basis with which to link agency services to public clients is produced. So the traditional model of writing regulations can be beneficial in one respect. But when applied to citizen-involvement programs, the situation can all too easily be perceived as regulating and co-opting opposition.

More fundamentally, regulations often encourage more administrative bureaucracy. Since citizen involvement is, in part, a reaction to a large centralized bureaucracy, writing regulations is like trying to cure the disease with more of the same. Writing regulations to deal with this centralization-decentralization control problem is not easy. Not all parts of the country view citizen participation similarly—even on similar issues. Those who write national regulations usually respond to pressures from national interest groups and to national issues and thus produce nationally oriented policy. When agency field personnel perceive that such policy conflicts with local needs, regulations can become either limiting or expanding. In short, the purpose of regulations can be subverted.

A good example of this is the recently enacted Citizen Advisory Committee Act, adopted by Congress, which requires formal approval by the Office of Management and Budget (OMB) before an agency employs a Citizens Advisory Committee (CAC). The act seeks to overcome the problem of unrepresentative advisory committees that are self-perpetuating and unnecessary.

How does an agency respond to this Act? Most CACs are established by agencies at the regional, state, or local levels to gain representative input or support for agency decisions that will be implemented at those levels. Should all such CACs be approved by OMB? If not, what are the rules for exceptions?

The idea that OMB should be the arbiter of such local efforts at responsive bureaucracy contradicts the decentralized nature of citizen involvement. An agency can choose to ignore the law on the grounds that local CAC efforts meet the responsive spirit of the law, or, as generally is the case, they write regulations.

In writing regulations, the agency first must decide on the CAC technique's appropriateness to a citizen-involvement program. Depending on the various field personnel, this easily can be interpreted as subverting and distrusting field professionals' judgment. On the other hand, the agency has a responsibility to assume that the national interest is met and it should not encourage disregard for national laws.

Assuming that the agency moves beyond this debate and writes regulations on CACs, what do they say? Most likely, the regulations will be filled with caveats about not using CACs and with careful procedures for approval. If, as is often the case, the agency has only general citizen-involvement regulations, such specific procedural guidelines easily can be used to justify very narrow interpretations of citizen involvement—despite national policy. Thus, a regulation necessitated by a national law that encourages responsive and representative government can be used by field personnel as an argument that the agency doesn't really desire citizen involvement. The norm becomes: Do only the minimum. Consequently, agency application of the regulation might do little to manage the problem of representativeness because of a myriad of control problems saddling its attempts at regulation.

There is another sense in which writing citizen-involvement regulations looks like curing the disease with more of the same. Frequently, regulations are written by lawyers or in legal terminology. They have a paralegal flavor to them. The formality and the strategies of conflict resolution encouraged by legalistic regulations can inhibit broad citizen-involvement efforts. Let me illustrate.

The injunction, which escalates project stoppage and litigation costs, is a very familiar syndrome. As a people, our willingness to go to court is testimony to our faith in the legal system. However, legal conflict resolution assumes two positions: for and against. Most of the players' energy goes to articulating positions for and against the issue. Those in the middle either move to the extreme or drop out, not to be heard. Writing legalistic regulations for citizen involvement can have the effect of building in this paradigm of conflict resolution before there is any conflict. Representation of mediating issues and values is decreased, and opportunities for middle-ground mediation are lost. Citizen-involvement goals of isolating extremes of conflicts and building the middle ground are lost.

Regulations concerning public hearings frequently fit this scenario. An air of formal legalisms such as "testimony" and "cross-examination" procedures abound. Such regulations can do more to solidify the extremes than to create options for negotiations. Rarely do they encourage dialogue beyond stating positions. Most information flows one way.

Although they are sometimes necessary, such hearings are more often misapplied citizen-involvement efforts. Even when formal public-hearing regulations are only part of a set of citizen-involvement regulations, they communicate this formalistic approach to conflict resolution. They may encourage staff who so desire to confirm the "us" and "them" syndrome. They may encourage closed management styles that result in loss of middle-ground negotiation points. Agency tendencies to control information flow selectively might be encouraged rather than reduced. Representativeness would then suffer.

Thus, regulation writing, however well motivated, can easily be counterproductive. Regulations frequently exacerbate representativeness problems by decreasing agency responsiveness. A key to avoiding this possibility is finding a balance between a level of abstraction and concrete specificity. That balance will be struck differently for different agencies, in part because they are organized differently. Whatever the balance, regulations should avoid excessive legalism and dogmatism. Options and regional innovations in application of technique need to be encouraged.

Disrupting the Agency Routine

Rarely does an agency's time frame for decision making fit that demanded by citizen involvement. Short-term agency decisions often require consensus, which takes too long to build. On the other hand, consensus built in through planning often deteriorates by the time specific implementation actions are taken by the agency. Does the agency change to fit citizen-involvement requirements, or does the agency try to make citizen involvement fit agency requirements? In either case, routine ways of doing agency business will be disrupted. But the search for some synthesis of these two questions is a major source of impact on the agency as it attempts to meet mandated requirements for citizen participation.

A first attempt to implement citizen involvement usually consists of hiring some new staff or consultants and establishing or assigning a branch or unit of the agency to carry out the citizen-participation requirement. Organizationally creating a separate citizen-involvement branch or specialist does legitimize the activity. It also facilitates management's perception that the activity can be controlled. Whether or not this is true, conflict is likely between this new, vaguely defined activity called citizen involvement and the established traditional public-affairs office. After all, what has the public-affairs office been doing if not facilitating agency-public contact?

Although it is often bitter, this conflict can be useful; that is, it forces further refinement in the agency's citizen-involvement definition and policy. But this refinement also breeds new conflict. Some of those newly recruited experts begin operating more closely with line professionals. Indeed, the distinction between technical expert and citizen-involvement specialist blurs. Consequently, fresh perspectives subtly work their way into line operations. Citizen-involvement activities move closer to line-operation responsibilities; that is, the study manager or facilities operator is less able to segment these activities.

As citizen-involvement activities increase, so, too, does the perceived direct stake of such people. In short, citizen-involvement activities become part of operating job responsibilities rather than just an externally managed, mysterious "black box." This shift in perception is painful and is not always accomplished. It is the point at which many agency personnel find themselves today.

A similar syndrome usually unfolds in early agency attempts to contract out citizen involvement. Putting the citizen-involvement package under a contract assumes a "black-box" approach. In other words, segment the citizen-involvement program and let the experts handle the analysis. However, if the citizen-involvement process questions the validity of assumptions, alternatives, or even the agency purpose, a monkey wrench is thrown into the decision gears. If the agency believes it should go back to reanalyze, it faces contractual problems in doing so. Is another contract written? Did the contractor fulfill the obligations of the first? In short, more administrative problems surface to confound the agency's attempts at responsiveness. Basically, there is an inherent problem of coordination when citizen involvement moves away from those vested with decisive authority. That is true with the public-affairs office in the conflict as well as with citizen involvement contractors.

Given the agency problem of adjustment and unfamiliarity with citizen involvement and associated analysis, what should be the policy? Outside consulting is useful and necessary, but such citizen-involvement consulting works best when experienced contractors act as consultants to agency staff. They can provide support, insight, and critique, but they cannot substitute for responsible decision makers. Once the decision-making authority and the citizen-involvement responsibility are separated, the effectiveness of the citizen-involvement program is weakened. But is it possible to sensitize various levels of agency decision makers to citizen-involvement techniques and programs?

After years of their developing managerial and technical expertise, the demand for citizen involvement can be a hard pill for agency officials to swallow. After all, should not the public-affairs experts take care of it? But when agency expertise becomes too routinized, it can subtly cross the line from expanding public options to limiting options. Expertise begins to look more like solutions seeking applications than like problem-solving capability. At this point, citizen involvement seriously impinges upon professional self-images and generates considerable dissonance among personnel.

Agencies frequently adopt new training and recruitment strategies to meet this dissonance. Realistically, an agency can neither retrain all old employees nor recruit all new ones; it usually develops some strategy between these extremes. But training for citizen involvement presents numerous problems as well as opportunities. Any concerted training/recruitment strategy to meet the dissonance problem assumes support strategies by the general management.

Obviously, training should be geared to target audiences. Middle-level managers make different decisions and have different needs than executive-level or line professionals. A training program must consider first the essential citizen-involvement message to be communicated across decision-making levels within the agency. This message can then be packaged to fit the specific needs of different decision makers.

More fundamentally, does the training proceed from the top down or the bottom up? Equipping line operators with citizen-involvement skills and encouraging their use is one thing. But to do this without management support will increase frustration and could alienate the personnel from the management. By the same token, sensitizing management to public-involvement needs and carrot/stick tools is useless without an implementation capability. So three critical training questions emerge: (1) How do I package the message for varying decision makers? (2) How do I phase the "top-down" and "bottom-up" approaches? and (3) Can I monitor my training impact?

One of the best approaches to citizen-involvement training is an interactive, learn-by-doing model. Such a hands-on approach builds confidence and experience. More than this, an interactive approach offers fascinating joint training opportunities; agency personnel can interact with state, local, and public-interest groups within the training format. Not only do such trainees develop public-involvement skills, but they build a basis for continued dialogue. Also, complex agency rules and limitations, often so hard to communicate publicly, become quickly understood within the interactive working environment. In effect, the joint citizen-involvement training itself becomes an effective public-involvement tool. The few agency attempts at this approach look promising.

Suggestions for Implementing
Citizen-Involvement Programs

The preceding discussion has identified four general approaches to implementing citizen-involvement programs: (1) writing regulations; (2) developing a training strategy; (3) developing an overall management strategy; and (4) hiring consultants. Obviously, these are not mutually exclusive, and it is likely that an agency will create a mix of these approaches as part of an overall strategy. In so doing, six major points are important to consider in creating an effective citizen-involvement strategy.

First, implementation of citizen-involvement programs must start by realizing that initial dissonance will arise. The roots of that dissonance and its likely effects must be understood and anticipated. Initial conflicts, such as between public-affairs offices and public-involvement staff, should be usefully managed. Overall management rewards should be commensurate with the way the staff actually allocates time. For example, if planners spend increasing time in coordination with local officials, are they still being rewarded only for quantity of computer output?

Second, decisions must be made about how much sharing of decision should be done and can be done. The "should" versus "can" distinction of these decisions is critical. Often staff analysis of the "can" in sharing comes packaged to executives as the "should" of decision sharing.

Third, citizen-involvement programs must be closely related to actual decision making. Either managers get into citizen-involvement programs or line-staff are given more decision authority. Agencies will find some point in between these extremes. At any rate, consultants should be used only as resources to consult. When outside consultants are given the responsibility for citizen involvement, decision makers become further isolated from the effects of their decisions. Consultants can provide critical staff support, training, evaluation, and critiques. But insofar as the success of citizen involvement depends on getting close to decisions, they should not replace decision makers.

Fourth, understanding and managing the decentralization-centralization conflict is extremely important. This is particularly true when writing regulations. Think about the counterintuitive or unexpected results of regulations. Avoid blind faith in regulations—but use them wisely.

Fifth, training is one of the best long-range techniques in implementing citizen-involvement programs. Training should be coupled to strategies of recruiting new personnel. It must also be keyed to varying audiences within the agency. Effective training programs require enough flexibility to change as the agency and issues change in the process. Interactive training models offer even further citizen-involvement opportunities. Joint training programs themselves can become citizen-involvement techniques.

Sixth, citizen-involvement techniques must be appropriate—in time and money—to the type of decision being made. As such, funding can become a major consideration in the successful citizen-involvement program. Citizen-involvement techniques must be clearly linked to the decision-making process. There is, of course, budgeting for line decision-making activities, such as interviews, advertising, press releases, hearings, large and small meetings, workshops, surveys and reports; but something called citizen-involvement funding is difficult to conceptualize. It is more difficult to trace professional staff time in design, concern and interaction for citizen involvement, because these attitudinal orientations should become part of the larger professional job definition.

Debates over percentage funding, such as 10 percent or 20 percent or 30 percent of program funds, are most relevant in initial implementation stages, as opposed to mature citizen-involvement programs. The goal is to move away from such program-level debate to specific cost discussion of line items to be used by agency professionals. Indeed, funding levels for specific techniques can change dramatically, depending on the specific context. For example, it is more expensive to bilingual or multilingual workshops than workshops in English. Despite variance, it is possible to develop some general approximations of costs of techniques, as illustrated in table 8-1.

Some Normative Guidelines

In addition to considering the six general points just identified, I have found a number of normative guidelines to be helpful in planning and implementing citizen-involvement programs:

1. Citizen involvement is not a technique; rather, it is a strategy, an approach, a philosophy. There is no one way to handle citizen involvement. Avoid the syndrome of a technique looking for an application; what works in one place will not always work in some other place. It is not the technique that is important so much as the people who employ the technique and their attitude.

2. Citizen involvement is not a substitute for the representative political process. In fact, it cannot be useful without complementing that process, but it will have an impact on that political process.

3. No one citizen-involvement program can claim to have "represented" the people. No planner should allow a citizen-involvement program exclusive sovereignty over his or her interpretation of the public will, but the program can be used to show competing views of that will.

4. Citizen involvement is not a panacea. More conflict will be generated, new time allocations and resource commitment will be required. But remember, the question is not how much citizen involvement will cost, but, more relevant, whether we can do anything at all without it.

5. Think of the positive contributions of citizen involvement—how it can supplement and improve other technical efforts. How will it make better decisions?

6. The goals of a citizen-involvement program and the roles of participants must be clearly defined.

Table 8-1
Rough Cost Guide to Most Frequently Used Public-Involvement Techniques

Technique	Cost ($)
Interviews (per 20-minute interview)	15-30
Newspaper advertising	250-750
Radio advertising	250-750
Press release	100-500
Public hearing	2,500-6,500
Large public meeting	2,500-6,500[a]
Small meeting or workshop	2,000-4,000[a]
Publicity on radio or TV	250-500
50-page report	5,000-10,000
200-page report	10,000-50,000
Information bulletins (4-8 pages)	500-1,500
Conducting a survey:	
Per mailed questionnaire	3-5
Per telephone interview	10-15
Per personal interview	15-30

Source: U.S. Army Corps of Engineers, *Executive Seminar Public Involvement in Water Resources Planning*, Institute for Water Resources, Ft. Belvoir, and Synergy Consultation Services, Cupertino, Calif., March 1978.
[a]May be reduced if a series of identical workshops or meetings is held.

7. Once started, be honest. Citizen involvement based on false assumptions and expectations of clever co-optation will be disastrous. Whether your efforts are honest can only be judged by you and your participants.

8. Be prepared to accept and implement decisions of the participants. Just be clear concerning what types of decisions both you and the participants in the citizen-involvement program should be making.

A Checklist of Questions

In answering the question of how an agency of the federal government can effectively implement a citizen-involvement program, this essay has raised a number of other related questions. Because no simple and universally applicable answers can be applied to every situation, the questions themselves take on an even more important significance. Accordingly, in closing, I should like to offer a checklist of questions that I have found helpful to consider in planning and implementing citizen-involvement programs:

1. What are the agency's management goals and objectives for citizen involvement? What are your citizen-involvement objectives?

2. What evaluation devices will be used to determine the success of your citizen-involvement programs?

3. Is there some visible way to gauge the ongoing progress of the program?

4. Has the history or background of the program been investigated? Who has been involved in the past? Have they been contacted?

5. Are there mechanisms within the program to deal with groups who will be significantly affected but are unlikely or unable to articulate concerns?

6. What resources other than immediate colleagues are available to assist in planning, implementing, and evaluating the program?

7. Who are the participating publics? Is a clear distinction made between the "information audience" and the "participating public"?

8. As the program progresses, is information published from time to time for responses to be effective?

9. What methods will be used to keep the public informed throughout the process?

10. Who is responsible for implementing the citizen-involvement plan? Do they know it? Are tasks specifically assigned?

11. Has the plan been reviewed with section chiefs, project manager, agency director? Were they included in the design, or did they review the draft only?

12. Does the plan reach out to a broad range of nontraditional publics, such as users, the affected, past problem groups, other technical help?

13. Do the techniques (or meeting formats) match your purposes at various program stages?

14. Does the program involve citizens on their own turf?

15. In reviewing your citizen-involvement plan, do all the activities actually deliver the goals and objectives you assigned them at various program stages?

16. Who are the new publics at each stage? Why? How will they be integrated into the program?

17. How will the effect of citizen comment on the program be demonstrated?

18. What funds and personnel are available to implement the program?

19. How will the plan account for the advice you will *not* be able to use and the concerns and value system you will *not* be able to protect?

20. How are public views being recorded and interpreted?

Acknowledgments and Bibliography

Much of the material discussed in this essay reflects the author's public-involvement training and program experience in the Army Corps of

Engineers and other federal agencies. The ideas are a collective product of numerous people, not the least of whom have been trainees. Specific note is due to Mr. James Creighton, formerly of Synergy Consultation Services of Saratoga, California; Mr. William Weidman of Synergy Consultation, San Diego, California; Mr. James Ragan, of Ragan Associates; Mr. James R. Hanchey of the Institute for Water Resources; Dr. Robert Wolfe, Office of Chief of Engineers; and the numerous federal agency employees and members of the Federal Interagency Council on Citizen Participation. Obviously the essay views are mine alone. They do not necessarily represent agency policy.

Specific documents used as source material for the essay are the following:

Creighton, James and William Weidman, *Citizen Participation/Public Involvement Staff Workbook* (Cupertino, Calif.: Synergy Consultation Services, February 1972).

Delli Priscoli, Jerry, *Why the Federal and Regional Interest in Public Involvement in Water Resources Development.* U.S. Army Corps of Engineers, Institute for Water Resources, Ft. Belvoir, Va., Working Paper 78-1, January 1978.

_____ , *Public Involvement and Social Impact Analysis: Union Looking for Marriage.* U.S. Army Corps of Engineers, Institute for Water Resources, Ft. Belvoir, Va., Working Paper 78-2, January 1978.

Federal Interagency Council on Citizen Participation. *Proceedings of the Conference on Citizen Participation in Government Decision Making,* Washington, D.C., December 1976.

Lasswell, Harold, *Politics: Who Gets What, When and How* (Gloucester, Mass.: Peter Smith, 1951).

Ragan, James R., *The Nuts and Bolts of Public Participation in Water Quality Planning: Skills Workbook* (Pacific Palisides, Calif.: James Ragan Associates, February 1978).

U.S. Army Corps of Engineers, Executive Seminar: *Public Involvement in Water Resources Planning Workbook,* Institute for Water Resources, Ft. Belvoir Va., and Synergy Consultation Services, Cupertino, Calif., March 1978.

U.S. Federal Regional Counsels and Community Services Administration, *Citizen Participation* (Washington: Government Printing Office, January 1978).

9 Matching Method to Purpose: The Challenges of Planning Citizen-Participation Activities

Judy B. Rosener

In the United States, the term *citizen participation* has been associated historically with periodic voting and with the many voluntary associations that so impressed deTocqueville in the early nineteenth century. Not until the "maximum feasible participation" clause of the Economic Opportunity Act of 1964 did citizen participation become an activity mandated by law in a large number of public programs. The fact that citizen-participation mandates continue to proliferate at all levels of government has made citizen participation an increasingly important issue to both citizens and public officials.

Unfortunately, those with responsibility for the design, implementation, and evaluation of mandated citizen-participation programs have been given little guidance. Most mandates are vague and ambiguous. Rarely do they contain hints as to what is expected. Standards by which participation should be measured are conspicuous by their absence. There is little consistency in the way participation is perceived; in the way participation programs are developed; in the way participation activities are carried out; and in the way participation evaluations are performed. Therefore, it is difficult to know what works and what doesn't; and opportunities to learn from the experience of others have been severely limited.

Lack of consistency in the design, implementation, and evaluation of participation programs, although unfortunate, is understandable. Citizen participation means different things to different people and even different things to the same people, depending on the issue, its timing, and the political setting in which it takes place. While there are no standard approaches to citizen participation that can be applied in different situations, all programs share the common need for planning. Unfortunately, planning is the Achilles' heel of many citizen-participation programs. Insufficient time and analysis are devoted to planning and, as a result, participation activities are selected arbitrarily. Although thorough planning is not the only factor contributing to the success of a citizen-participation program, it is the initial and unavoidable step and an extremely important one.

Conceptualizing the Citizen-Participation Issue

How can citizen-participation planning be addressed effectively? The first task is to conceptualize the citizen-participation issue. Just what are we trying to accomplish when we acknowledge the need to involve citizens in some aspect of the public-policy process? Conceptualizing the issue means asking the simple questions of *who, what, where, how,* and *when*?

1. Who are the parties to be involved in citizen participation?
2. What are the specific functions we wish to have performed by this participation program?
3. Where do we wish the participation road to lead?
4. How should citizens be involved?
5. When in the policy process is participation needed or desired?

These are simple questions, yet rarely are they asked prior to the development of a citizen-participation program. More often, it is assumed that all parties, that is, elected officials, affected citizens, and public administrators, will be equally served by some participation activity; that all participation activities perform the same kinds of functions; or that all phases of the public-policy process require the same kind or amount of citizen involvement. Because there tends to be a lack of awareness of the very complex nature of the participation concept, participation techniques that are simple and inexpensive and that ensure that control will be maintained are chosen over and over again by public officials who don't know what else to do, or who are threatened by the possibility of losing control over outcomes. Rather than spending time thinking about purposes of participation, and what methods might best serve those purposes, public officials too frequently spend their time carrying out participation activities that fail to satisfy citizens, themselves, or the intent of the participation mandates.

The Need for Goals and Objectives

What public officials should realize is that citizen participation is like a professional sport. It takes place in a public forum where there is competition between individuals and groups with conflicting goals; where the individuals and groups that participate play different roles at different times; where the playing conditions change from time to time; where the planning of strategies is a major activity; where no one group wins every contest; and where there is an ongoing need to evaluate performance in order to succeed. Like the owner of a professional ball club, the designer of a citizen-participation program needs to think about goals and objectives, about options and plays, resources and timing, strategy and performance. And, like planning for a successful sports season, planning for a successful participation program involves a great deal of thought and analysis prior to the first public performance.

The planning that accompanies the design of any participation program should first include a determination of goals and objectives. For example:

1. Is the participation intended to generate ideas?
2. Is it to identify attitudes?
3. Is it to disseminate information?
4. Is it to resolve some identified conflict?
5. Is it to measure opinion?
6. Is it to review a proposal?
7. Or is it merely to serve as a safety valve for pent-up emotions?

The list of possible participation objectives will differ from time to time and from issue to issue. Therefore, when a specific mandated program is required, it is important to determine which objectives are most relevant. Once the goals and objectives of citizen participation in any given instance are delineated, it becomes clear that participation is perceived differently depending on the type of issue, the parties involved, the policy process, and the attitudes of the public officials and citizens who will be involved. If differences in perception and expectations are not identified at the outset, and realistic objectives are not made clear, the expectations of those involved in the participation program will not have been met and they will become disenchanted. If, on the other hand, in the design of a citizen-participation program, objectives and the parties to be served by them are clearly identified, it will be possible to develop a program with which expectations will be met. When this is done, it will be possible to evaluate specific participation activities, since they can be measured against the objective they were expected to achieve.

Problems in Establishing Citizen-Participation
Goals and Objectives

One of the stumbling blocks to the kind of analysis that is necessary in the design of an effective participation program is the difficulty associated with the articulation of participation goals and objectives. Yet it is this articulation that forms the basis of any wise choice of participation methods. The difficulty in determining goals, objectives, and techniques may be caused by confusion over what is meant by the terms. Therefore, awareness of the meaning of the following terms may be useful in planning a citizen participation program.

A *goal* is nothing more than a generalized statement of intended accomplishment.[1] It is usually abstract and somewhat ambiguous.

An *objective* is more specific. It is a statement of the changes or conditions that some activity is expected to produce; put another way, it is a function to be performed.

A *technique* or method is a vehicle by which an objective is to be achieved.

As an illustration of how these different terms are applied, consider the following example of a plan to meet the participation mandates of Title I of the Housing and Community Development Act of 1974. One goal of the participation program might be "to meet the mandate of the Act." Another might be "to develop trust in the political system." The objectives would be the functions to be performed in order to "meet the mandate" and "develop trust." In the case of this Act, the participation objectives are clearly spelled out:

Citizens must be provided with adequate information concerning the amount of funds available for proposed community development and housing activities, the range of activities which may be undertaken, and other important program requirements. . . . Citizens must also be given adequate opportunity to articulate needs, express preferences about proposed activities, assist in the selection of priorities and otherwise participate in the development of the application.[2]

Thus, the objectives would be: (1) to disseminate information, (2) to solicit and identify the attitudes and opinions of affected groups, (3) to facilitate participation, (4) to generate new ideas and alternatives, and (5) to establish priorities. These objectives would be the functions to be performed by some set of participation activities. They are the participation purposes to which some participation technique or method will be matched.

Why Citizen Participation Planning Is Often Inadequate

When participation goals and objectives are not clearly articulated and participating parties have different expectations of what participation is to achieve, it is not possible to measure the effectiveness of any participation activity, because there is lack of agreement as to what the participation is intended to do. In light of the vital importance of establishing clear goals and objectives in the planning process, it is important to understand why this task is so often done inadequately.

One of the reasons that citizen-participation planning is often inadequate is that many public officials find citizens a "professional hazard." The involvement of citizens is viewed as being time-consuming, inefficient, irrational, and not very productive. So because they work under tight time and financial constraints, public officials tend not to focus attention on citizen participation until forced to do so. By keeping the purposes of participation unclear, they can always claim success. However, when a participation mandate clearly states objectives, such as in the case cited earlier, then public officials have less discretion over what participation activities will be undertaken, and they will need to plan activities that are directly related to the stated objectives. In most instances, however, objectives are not spelled out, and ambiguity reigns. Thus citizens are frustrated, and public officials are confused, because they don't understand why the citizens are frustrated.

Another reason that the planning of citizen participation is often inadequate is that citizen participation is a complex concept; it takes a great deal of thought to design an effective participation program. Planning for effective participation, as we have noted, requires an analysis of the kind and nature of the issue that is to be addressed, the individuals or groups that are to be affected, the resources that will be needed, and the goals and objectives for which the participation is being requested or required. Planning for effective participation necessitates making a distinction between citizen participation as an end in itself, and participation as a means to an end. It necessitates deciding on whether short- or long-term interests are at stake. It means agreeing on legislative intent. It means attempting to ascertain what the "participation costs" will be, and how an issue will be understood by those willing to pay the costs. Good planning for citizen participation requires careful analysis.

A final and related reason for the frequency of poor planning is that planning for participation by citizens needs considerable time prior to the taking of any visible action. This time is often difficult to justify to those who are unaware of the complexity of the participation concept. It is this time, however, which is crucial to the proper planning of any participation activity. When sufficient time is allowed to analyze issues, participants, resources, and participation goals and objectives prior to the choosing of participation techniques, the chance of program success is greatly enhanced. While it may seem easier and less time consuming to "snatch a technique" and "go through the motions," in the long run this will be counterproductive. Poorly planned participation programs create a lack of confidence in government and generate a stronger demand by citizens for the monitoring of governmental activities.

On Matching Method to Purpose

We have concentrated our attention on the critical importance of clearly identifying goals and objectives in planning for citizen participation, but it is also necessary to analyze the various techniques or methods that are available, their track record, and the resources they require.[3] The often-heard cry, "We can't get the citizens to participate," is all too frequently related to the fact that the participation techniques selected by public officials are inappropriate and unsuited to program objectives and the capability of citizens. So while public officials claim apathy, citizens claim inequity. It is essential, therefore, in planning for citizen participation to select methods that meet objectives and are within the resource capabilities of the government agencies and citizens that will be involved.

Assuming that the goals and objectives of a participation program have been articulated, where does one go to find out about the methods and technique that also need analysis? In the last few years, there have been a number of efforts to accumulate knowledge about various participation techniques, along with attempts to decribe the different functions these techniques perform.[4] Suggestions for the matching of tecnniques to function have also appeared, particularly in the literature of transportation planning.[5] In the areas of social service and land-use planning, there are also studies of specific participation techniques and evaluations of their effectiveness.[6] The applicability of these studies is somewhat limited, because of the variability of the factors associated with the programs, but they do provide some helpful insights in regard to alternative techniques.

In addition to these resources, the reader may find the matrix and list of techniques at the close of this essay (see table 9-1) helpful in considering how different techniques can be matched to various participation functions or techniques. It does not provide information about the resources needed in the use of any of the techniques. It does not indicate where in the policy process a given technique works best. It is merely an attempt to conceptualize participation in terms of purpose and method. Anyone using the matrix will necessarily have to consider timing, the kind and complexity of an issue, the quantity and quality of resources available to public officials and citizens, community characteristics, the political climate, and other factors affecting the determination of which technique to use.

The Steps to Successful Participation Planning

This essay has described a number of elements in citizen-participation planning. When thought of in a direct and practical way, it may be helpful to consider these elements as steps in planning and implementing a citizen-participation program. The steps are:

1. Identify the individuals or groups who will or should be involved in the participation program being planned.
2. Decide where in the policy process the identified parties should participate; that is, policy development, policy implementation, policy evaluation, or some combination thereof.
3. Articulate the participation goals and objectives in relation to all parties who will be involved; that is, the elected officials, the public administrators, the affected citizens.
4. Identify participation methods or techniques that could serve as vehicles for the achievement of participation goals and objectives.
5. Analyze the resources required by program administrators and participating citizens for any given technique or techniques.
6. Match alternative methods to objectives in terms of the resources available to the participating parties.
7. Select an appropriate method or methods to be used in the achievement of the specified objectives.
8. Implement the chosen participation activities.
9. Evaluate the implemented methods to see to what extent they achieved the articulated goals and objectives.

It is not suggested that taking the nine proposed steps will automatically ensure success, but it can be claimed that the process will minimize failure. Taking these steps will increase the possibility that basic assumptions and values upon which a participation program rests will be known to all those participating. Only when this happens will participation expectations be reasonable. It is the gap between expectations and results that so often leads to the questioning of the value of citizen participation. It is the contention of this essay that proper attention to the design of citizen-participation programs, the matching of method to purpose, should go a long way toward closing the gap between expectations and results.

Table 9-1
Technique/Function Matrix and Descriptions

Technique	Function													
	Identify Attitudes and Opinions	Identify Impacted Groups	Solicit Impacted Groups	Facilitate Participation	Clarify Planning Process	Answer Citizen Questions	Disseminate Information	Generate New Ideas and Alternatives	Facilitate Advocacy	Promote Interaction Between Interest Grps.	Resolve Conflict	Plan Program and Policy Review	Change Attitudes Toward Government	Develop Support/Minimize Opposition
Arbitration and Mediation Planning	X							X		X	X			
Charrette	X			X	X	X		X		X	X	X	X	X
Citizen's Advisory Committee	X			X	X	X		X			X	X	X	X
Citizen Employment	X		X	X	X	X	X	X						X
Citizen Honoraria			X	X	X	X	X				X	X	X	X
Citizen Referendum	X											X	X	
Citizen Representatives on Policy-Making Bodies	X			X	X			X					X	X
Citizen Review Board				X								X		X
Citizen Surveys	X		X											
Citizen Training				X	X				X				X	
Community Technical Assistance	X			X	X			X	X					
Computer-based Techniques	depends on specific technique chosen													
Coordinator or Coordinator-Catalyst	X			X	X	X				X	X		X	X
Design-In	X	X		X	X	X		X				X	X	X
Drop-In Centers		X		X	X	X						X	X	X
Fishbowl Planning				X	X	X	X	X			X	X	X	X
Focused Group Interview	X		X	X		X				X				
Game Simulations					X					X	X	X		X
Group Dynamics										X	X		X	
Hotline		X		X		X								

| Interactive Cable TV |
| Media-based Issue Balloting |
| Meetings—Community-Sponsored |
| Meetings—Neighborhood |
| Meetings—Open Informational |
| Neighborhood Planning Council |
| Ombudsman |
| Open Door Policy |
| Planning Balance Sheet |
| Policy Capturing |
| Policy Delphi |
| Priority-Setting Committee |
| Public Hearing |
| Public Information Programs |
| Random Selected Participation Groups |
| Short Conference |
| Task Forces |
| Value Analysis |
| Workshops |

Table 9-1 (cont.)

Description of Functions

Identify Attitudes and Opinions: determine community and/or interest group feelings and priorities.

Identify Impacted Groups: determine which groups will be directly or indirectly affected by policy and planning decisions.

Solicit Impacted Groups: invite the individuals and groups thought to be impacted by the program to participate in the planning process.

Facilitate Participation: make it easy for individuals and groups to participate.

Clarify Planning Process: explain or otherwise inform the public on planning, policies, projects, or processes.

Answer Citizen Questions: provide the opportunity for citizen or group representatives to ask questions.

Disseminate Information: transmit information to the public; includes techniques which provide access to information.

Generate New Ideas and Alternatives: provide the opportunity for citizens or group representatives to suggest alternatives or new ideas.

Facilitate Advocacy: provide assistance in developing and presenting a particular point of view or alternative.

Promote Interaction between Interest Groups: bring interest group representatives together for exchange of views.

Resolve Conflict: mediate and resolve interest group differences.

Plan, Program, and Policy Review: provide an opportunity for policies to be reviewed.

Change Attitudes toward Government: makes individuals or groups view government differently.

Develop Support/Minimize Opposition: explain the costs, benefits, and tradeoffs to the public, thereby defusing possible opposition and building support.

Participation Techniques

Arbitration and Mediation Planning: Utilization of labor-management mediation and arbitration techniques to settle disputes between interest groups in the planning process.

Charrette: Process which convenes interest groups (governmental and non-governmental) in intensive interactive meetings lasting from several days to several weeks.

Citizen Advisory Committees: A generic term used to denote any of several techniques in which citizens are called together to represent the ideas and attitudes of various groups and/or communities.

Citizen Employment: Concept involves the direct employment of *client* representatives; results in continuous input of clients' values and interests to the policy and planning process.

Table 9-1 (cont.)

Citizen Honoraria: Originally devised as an incentive for participation of low-income citizens. Honoraria differs from reimbursement for expenses in that it dignifies the status of the citizen and places a value on his/her participation.

Citizen Referendum: A statutory technique whereby proposed public measures or policies may be placed before the citizens by a ballot procedure for approval/disapproval or selection of one of several alternatives.

Citizen Representation on Public Policy-Making Bodies: Refers to the composition of public policy-making boards either partially or wholly of appointed or elected citizen representatives.

Citizen Review Board: Technique in which decision-making authority is delegated to citizen representatives who are either elected or appointed to sit on a review board with the authority to review alternative plans and decide which plan should be implemented.

Citizen Surveys of Attitudes and Opinions: Only technique other than talking with *every* citizen that is statistically representative of *all* citizens; allows for no interaction between citizens and planners.

Citizen Training: Technique facilitates participation through providing citizens with information and planning and/or leadership training, e.g., game simulation, lecture, workshops, etc.

Community Technical Assistance: A generic term covering several techniques under which interest groups are given professional assistance in developing and articulating alternative plans or objections to agency proposed plans and policies. Some specific techniques are:

Advocacy Planning: Process whereby affected groups employ professional assistance directly with private funds and consequently have a client-professional relationship.

Community Planning Center: Groups independently plan for their community using technical assistance employed by and responsible to a community-based citizens group.

Direct Funding to Community Groups: Similar process to Advocacy Planning, however, funding comes from a government entity.

Plural Planning: Technique whereby each interest group has its own planner (or group of planners) with which to develop a proposed plan based on the group's goals and objectives.

Computer-based Techniques: A generic term describing a variety of experimental techniques which utilize computer technology to enhance citizen participation.

Coordinator or Coordinator-Catalyst: Technique vests responsibility for providing a focal point for citizen participation in a project with a single individual. Coordinator remains in contact with all parties and channels feedback into the planning process.

Design-In: Refers to a variety of planning techniques in which citizens work with maps, scale representations, and photographs to provide a better idea of the effect on their community of proposed plans and projects.

Drop-In Centers: Manned information distribution points where a citizen can stop in to ask questions, review literature, or look at displays concerning a project affecting the area in which the center is located.

120

Table 9-1 (cont.)

Fishbowl Planning: A planning process in which all parties can express their support or opposition to an alternative before it is adopted, thereby bringing about a restructuring of the plan to the point where it is acceptable to all. Involves use of several participatory techniques—public meetings, public brochures, workshops, and a citizens' committee.

Focused Group Interviews: Guided interview of six to 10 citizens in which individuals are exposed to others' ideas and can react to them; based on the premise that more information is available from a group than from members individually.

Game Simulations: Primary focus is on experimentation in a risk-free environment with various alternatives (policies, programs, plans) to determine their impacts in a simulated environment where there is no actual capital investment and no real consequences at stake.

Group Dynamics: A generic term referring to either interpersonal techniques and exercises to facilitate group interaction or problem-solving techniques designed to highlight substantive issues.

Hotline: Used to denote any publicized phone answering system connected with the planning process. Hotlines serve two general purposes: 1) as an avenue for citizens to phone in questions on a particular project or policy and receive either a direct answer or an answer by return call; or 2) as a system whereby the citizen can phone and receive a recorded message.

Interactive Cable TV-based Participation: An experimental technique utilizing two-way coaxial cable TV to solicit immediate citizen reaction; this technique is only now in the initital stages of experimentation on a community level.

Media-based Issue Balloting: Technique whereby citizens are informed of the existence and scope of a public problem, alternatives are described, and then citizens are asked to indicate their views and opinions.

Meetings—Community-sponsored: Organized by a citizen group or organization; these meetings focus upon a particular plan or project with the objective to provide a forum for discussion of various interest group perspectives.

Meetings—Neighborhood: Held for the residents of a specific neighborhood that has been, or will be, affected by a specific plan or project, and usually are held either very early in the planning process or when the plans have been developed.

Meetings—Open Informational (also "Public Forum"): Meetings which are held voluntarily by an agency to present detailed information on a particular plan or project at any time during the process.

Neighborhood Planning Council: A technique for obtaining participation on issues which affect a specific geographic area; council serves as an advisory body to the public agency in identifying neighborhood problems, formulating goals and priorities, and evaluating and reacting to the agency's proposed plans.

Ombudsman: An independent, impartial administrative officer who serves as a mediator between citizen and government to seek redress for complaints, to further understanding of each other's position, or to expedite requests.

Open Door Policy: Technique involves encouragement of citizens to visit a local project office at any time on a "walk in" basis; facilitates direct communication.

Table 9-1 (cont.)

Planning Balance Sheet: Application of an evaluation methodology that provides for the assessment and rating of project alternatives according to the weighted objectives of local interest groups, as determined by the groups themselves.

Policy Capturing: A highly sophisticated, experimental technique involving mathematical models of policy positions of parties-at-interest. Attempts to make explicit the weighting and trading-off patterns of an individual or group.

Policy Delphi: A technique for developing and expressing the views of a panel of individuals on a particular subject. Initiated with the solicitation of written views on a subject, successive rounds of presented arguments and counter-arguments work toward consensus of opinion, or clearly established positions and supporting arguments.

Priority-setting Committees: Narrow-scope citizen group appointed to advise a public agency of community priorities in community development projects.

Public Hearings: Usually required when some major governmental program is about to be implemented or prior to passage of legislation; characterized by procedural formalities, an official transcript or record of the meeting, and its being open to participation by an individual or representative of a group.

Public Information Program: A general term covering any of several techniques utilized to provide information to the public on a specific program or proposal, usually over a long period of time.

Random Selected Participation Groups: Random selection within a statistical cross-section of groups such as typical families or transit-dependent individuals which meet on a regular basis and provide local input to a study or project.

Short Conference: Technique typically involves intensive meetings organized around a detailed agenda of problems, issues, and alternatives with the objective of obtaining a complete analysis from a balanced group of community representatives.

Task Force: An *ad hoc* citizen committee sponsored by an agency in which the parties are involved in a clearly-defined task in the planning process. Typical characteristics are small size (8-20), vigorous interaction between task force and agency, weak accountability to the general public, and specific time for accomplishment of its tasks.

Value Analysis: technique which involves various interest groups in the process of subjectively ranking consequences of proposals and alternatives.

Workshops: Working sessions which provide a structure for parties to discuss thoroughly a technical issue or idea and try to reach an understanding concerning its role, nature, and/or importance in the planning process.

Source: Reprinted from Judy B. Rosener, "A Cafeteria of Techniques and Critiques," *Public Management* 57, no. 12 (December 1975) by special permission. © 1975 by the International City Management Association.

Notes

1. Although there is no single definition of a goal or objective, the "generalized statement" definition is an accepted one. For a good discussion of goals and objectives, see Robert F. Mager, *Goal Analysis* (Belmont, Calif.: Fearson, 1972).

2. Community Services Administration, *Citizen Participation* (Washington: Community Services Administration, January 7, 1978), p. 101.

3. For a good discussion of how to evaluate resources when deciding on participation techniques, see Wayne R. Torrey and Florence W. Mills, "Selecting Effective Citizen Participation Techniques," *Transportation Research Board Manuscript* (Washington: Office of Program and Policy Planning, Federal Highway Administration, n.d.).

4. U.S. Federal Highway Administration, *Effective Citizen Participation in Transportation Planning,* Volume II, A catalog of techniques (Washington: U.S. Department of Transportation); Marvin L. Manheim and John H. Suhrbier, *A Catalogue of Community Interaction Techniques,* Transportation and Community Values Report No. 72110 (Cambridge, Mass.: Massachusetts Institute of Technology); Douglas C. Smith, Robert C. Stuart, and Robert Hanson, *Manual for Community Involvement in Highway Planning and Design* (Blacksburg, Va.: Center for Urban and Regional Studies, Virginia Polytechnic Institute and State University, May, 1975); Patricia Marshall, ed., "Citizen Participation Certification Techniques and Processes," in *Citizen Participation Certification for Community Development: A Reader on the Citizen Participation Process* (National Association of Housing and Redevelopment Officials, February, 1977); Robert and Mary Kweit, "The Search for Effective Citizen Participation," Paper delivered at the 1978 annual meeting of the American Society for Public Administration at Phoenix, Arizona.

5. U.S. Federal Highway Administration, *Effective Citizen Participation in Transportation Planning,* Volumes I and II.

6. Marshall, "Citizen Participation Certification"; Melvin Mogulof, *Citizen Participation: A Review and Commentary on Federal Policies and Practices* (Washington: The Urban Institute, January, 1970); Hans B.C. Spiegel, ed., "Citizen Participation in Federal Programs: A Review," *Journal of Voluntary Action Research,* Monograph No. L (1971); Richard Cole, *Citizen Participation and the Urban Policy Process* (Lexington, Mass.: Lexington Books, D.C. Heath and Company, 1974); Daniel P. Moynihan, *Maximum Feasible Misunderstanding* (New York: The Free Press, 1969); Nelson Rosenbaum, *Citizen Involvement,* in *Land Use Governance* (Washington: The Urban Institute, 1976).

About the Contributors

Barry Checkoway is an assistant professor, Department of Urban and Regional Planning, University of Illinois at Urbana-Champagne.

Jon Van Til is an associate professor and department chairman, Department of Urban Studies and Community Development, Rutgers University at Camden, New Jersey; he is also president of the Association of Voluntary Action Scholars.

Nelson Rosenbaum is a senior research associate at the Urban Institute, Washington, D.C.

David Cohen is president of Common Cause, Washington, D.C.

Janice E. Perlman is an associate professor of city and regional planning, University of California at Berkeley.

Walter A. Rosenbaum is a professor of political science at the University of Florida at Gainesville.

Jerry Delli Priscoli is a social scientist with the U.S. Army Corps of Engineers.

Judy B. Rosener is a member of the faculty of the Graduate School of Administration of the University of California at Irvine, and is a member of the California Coastal Commission.

About the Editor

Stuart Langton is the Lincoln Filene Professor of Citizenship and Public Affairs, Tufts University, Medford, Massachusetts. In his role as Lincoln Filene Professor, Mr. Langton provides general intellectual leadership to the work of the Lincoln Filene Center for Citizenship and Public Affairs. He has also served as a consultant to more than 100 government agencies and voluntary organizations.